Legal Writing in the Disciplines

Legal Writing in the Disciplines

A Guide to Legal Writing Mastery

Teri A. McMurtry-Chubb

MERCER UNIVERSITY
WALTER F. GEORGE SCHOOL OF LAW

CAROLINA ACADEMIC PRESS

Durham, North Carolina

Library of Congress Cataloging-in-Publication Data

McMurtry-Chubb, Teri A.
 Legal writing in the disciplines : a guide to legal writing mastery / Teri A. Mc-
Murtry-Chubb.
   p. cm.
 Includes index.
 ISBN 978-1-59460-959-6 (alk. paper)
 1. Legal composition. 2. Legal research--United States. I. Title.

 KF250.M39 2011
 808.06'634--dc23

                         2011040512

Carolina Academic Press
700 Kent Street
Durham, North Carolina 27701
Telephone (919) 489-7486
Fax (919) 493-5668
www.cap-press.com

Printed in the United States of America

For Dad and Ruth

Contents

Preface

Entering law school is like entering a foreign country for the first time. New law students do not know the language but only a few fancy catch phrases to get them through each day. Despite the friendly faces and helpful advice of second and third year law students, more seasoned travelers, new law students must figure out the terrain on their own. Professors can serve as guides, but the students must travel the journey themselves.

Legal writing serves as the passport to the legal arena. Without the ability to translate complex legal theories into clear and concise writing, lawyers cannot fully participate in the legal system. Bad legal writing is the equivalent of screaming English at someone who is not familiar with the language. The end result is the same. The screamer is amazed that their best efforts to communicate have failed. The listener smiles politely but remains totally ignorant of what the screamer attempts to communicate. Each walks away from the conversation frustrated and misunderstood.

Unfortunately, many law professors have become like the screamer in the previous paragraph in their approach to law teaching. Instead of meeting new law students at the point where they ended their undergraduate or graduate studies, we expect them to abandon their discipline-specific methodological thinking in favor of undefined, unexplored, and unexplained methodological approaches to the study of law. Most law professors do not seek to meet the students at the point of their last educational experience or to translate legal methodologies into a student's existing disciplinary methodological framework.

This misstep is also true of legal writing professionals who, despite creativity and enthusiasm in the classroom, continuously attempt to find a singular disciplinary methodological experience from which to teach legal analysis and writing. Because the analytical piece of legal writing is rooted in rule-based reasoning, many legal writing professors will seek examples of rule-based reasoning as they occur in the sciences and mathematics to analogize to legal analysis.[1] Likewise, some professors draw examples from the deductive and inductive reasoning models used in philosophy to demonstrate how logical, structured rule-based reasoning should occur in legal writing. Still, others find examples in rhetoric to demonstrate writing for a particular audience and argument construction. None of these approaches is incorrect. The flaw in their use is that it is not comprehensive. Those professors who have strong math backgrounds may use mathematical models to demonstrate rule-based reasoning, but those students in the class without strong math backgrounds have no point of reference. The same is true for any other singular disciplinary methodological source that a professor may use to analogize to legal analysis. Those who have a frame of reference can translate legal writing instruction into the familiar disciplinary framework. Everyone else cannot.

In any law school classroom, there are students from the social sciences, humanities, arts, sciences, and business. As legal educators, we should make legal education available to students at these various points of disciplinary access. This is especially true of legal writing professors. Most of the work done by attorneys is conducted through the exchange of paper. Thus, an effective lawyer must master the art of communication through writing. Without this skill, an attorney's conversations with the client, opposing counsel, and the court end prematurely. With this skill, the attorney can provide the client, opposing counsel, and the court with a roadmap to the desired legal destination. The goal of this text is to teach students how to draw that roadmap.

---

1. Karen L. Koch, *A Multidisciplinary Comparison of Rules-Driven Writing: Similarities in Legal Writing, Biology Research Articles, and Computer Programming*, 55 J. Legal Educ. (2005).

Copyright Permissions

The following publications are reprinted on the CD-ROM accompanying this text at the permission of the author(s), publication, and/or other person holding the copyright:

Chapter One:

Robert Clinton, *Figure 1: Diagram of Court Hierarchies and the American Legal System* (on file with the author).

Kevin Marshall & Juanda Daniel, PRINCIPLES OF CONTRACT LAW, *Table of Contents*; §§ 1–2 (2011).

Chapter Two:

Jane Eckett, *Hol(e)y Statues: Some reflections on holes, emptiness and longing in the work of two Australian émigré sculptors of the fifties*, PHILAMENT (Dec. 2009), http://sydney.edu.au/arts/publications/philament/issue15_contents.htm.

Chapter Three:

J.A. Martino, *Billy Pilgrim's Motion Sickness: Chronesthesia and Duration in Slaughterhouse-Five*, PHILAMENT (Aug. 2010), http://sydney.edu.au/arts/publications/philament/issue16_contents.htm.

Jane Eckett, *Hol(e)y Statues: Some reflections on holes, emptiness and longing in the work of two Australian émigré sculptors of the fifties*, PHILAMENT (Dec. 2009), http://sydney.edu.au/arts/publications/philament/issue15_contents.htm.

John Drury, *'The Elijah who was to come': Matthew's use of Malachi (Matt 11:2–15)* (on file with the author).

Frank Fury, *The Off-"Beat" Rhythms and Self-Expression in the Typography and Verse of Ntozake Shange*, PHILAMENT (Apr. 2004), http://sydney.edu.au/arts/publications/philament/issue3_contents.htm.

Brian McCabe, John Donne's *Via Media* in 'Satire III' (on file with the author).

Chapter Five:

Ralph Budwig (permission grantor), Prediction and Measurement of Volume Flow Rate (Mar. 2, 1999) (lab notebook on file with the permission grantor).

Zack Swider, Cross Cannizzaro Reaction: Synthesis of p-Chlorobenzyl Alcohol (Feb. 4, 2009) (lab report on file with the author).

Zack Swider, The Synthesis of Lydocaine (Jan. 28, 2009–Feb. 11, 2009) (lab report on file with the author).

Chapter Six:

Keely Byrne & Jim Detert, *Considering Profits and Principles in Technology Adoption Decisions (A)*, BUSINESS ROUNDTABLE INSTITUTE FOR CORPORATE ETHICS (2006), http://www.darden.virginia.edu/corporate-ethics/pdf/BRI-1003A.pdf.

Keely Byrne & Jim Detert, *Considering Profits and Principles in Technology Adoption Decisions (B)*, BUSINESS ROUNDTABLE INSTITUTE FOR CORPORATE ETHICS (2006), http://www.darden.virginia.edu/corporate-ethics/pdf/BRI-1003B.pdf.

The following publications are reprinted on the CD-ROM accompanying this text by permission granted through Creative Commons Attribution 2.0 Generic License (http://creativecommons.org/licenses/by/2.0/) unless otherwise specified:

Chapter One:

Figure 2: U.S. Court of Appeals and District Court Map, http://en.wikipedia.org/wiki/File:US_Court_of_Appeals_and_District_Court_map.svg, (licensed under a Creative Commons Attribution-Share Alike 2.5 Generic license: http://creativecommons.org/licenses/by-sa/2.5/deed.en).

Chapter Two:

Jeff A. Gow, *The adequacy of policy responses to the treatment needs of South Africans living with HIV (1999–2008)*, JOURNAL OF THE INTERNATIONAL AIDS SOCIETY (Dec. 14, 2009), http://www.jiasociety.org/content/12/1/37.

Edward J. López, *Congressional Trends to Tax and Spend: Examining Fiscal Voting Across Time and Chamber*, 1 THE OPEN POLITICAL SCIENCE JOURNAL 38–43 (2008).

Marie-Antoinette Sossou, *We Do Not Enjoy Equal Political Rights: Ghanaian Women's Perceptions on Political Participation in Ghana*, SAGE OPEN (2011), http://sgo.sagepub.com/content/early/2011/05/02/2158244011410715.full.

Chapter Three:

Mark Alan Graber & Abraham David Graber, *Get Your Paws Off of My Pixels: Personal Identity and Avatars as Self*, JOURNAL OF MEDICAL INTERNET RESEARCH (2010), http://www.jmir.org/2010/3/e28/.

Chapter Five:

Edwin van Dellen et al., *Long-Term Effects of Temporal Lobe Epilepsy on Local Neural Networks: A Graph Theoretical Analysis of Corticography Recordings.* THE PUBLIC LIBRARY OF SCIENCE (Nov. 26, 2009), http://www.plosone.org/article/info%3Adoi%2F10.1371%2Fjournal.pone.0008081.

Simon Reinke et al., *The Influence of Recovery and Training Phases on Body Composition, Peripheral Vascular Function and Immune System [sic] of Professional Soccer Players*, THE PUBLIC LIBRARY OF SCIENCE (Mar. 18, 2009), http://www.plosone.org/article/info%3Adoi%2F10.1371%2Fjournal.pone.0004910.

Acknowledgments

Thanks to God, without whom nothing in my life would be possible. Thanks to my husband, Mark Anthony Chubb, whose belief in me encourages my own faith. My research assistant, Daniela Oliva, and the Interlibrary Loan librarian, James Wiseman, are beyond compare. I give my heartfelt thanks to them for acquiring and compiling the voluminous amount of research necessary to create this book. My special thanks go to my writing specialists and proofreaders for this book, Diana Luu and Brian McCabe. Their hard work and dedication made this book better than I could have made it on my own. Funding for this project was provided by generous grants from the University of La Verne and the University of La Verne College of Law, respectively. Thanks to Mel Weresh for encouraging me while this work was in its early stages, and to Ralph Brill and Cassandra Hill for encouraging me while this work was in its later stages. Lastly, I thank Ron Riggins for his visionary leadership of Fairhaven College of Interdisciplinary Studies and for serving as one of my mentors. My tenure at Fairhaven College and the students I encountered there allowed me to shift my perspective on the law, legal analysis, and legal writing enough for me to conceive this book.

Introduction

The "myth of transience" is the widely held belief among the academy "that if we can do x, y, and z, the problem [of poor student writing] will be solved—in five years, ten years, or a generation—and higher education will be able to return to its real work."[2] Ultimately, law schools want an easy solution to the challenges facing novice legal writers without examining the institutional and structural barriers to student writing success. Not the least of these is the perception that legal education is a "free for all," accessible to students of any major. This perception denies the existence of law as a discipline, a discourse community, into which students must be integrated. Integration into any discourse community primarily occurs through reading and writing.

This book is a book of translation for new legal writers. Its purpose is to re-conceptualize law in its disciplinary context and to give both students and professors some tools to serve as a bridge between discourse communities, the legal discourse community, and various undergraduate and graduate discourse communities. The attempt of legal education to take students out of their disciplinary contexts (undergraduate and/or graduate) and place them into another (the legal discourse community) without context or explanation is problematic and leads to many of the frustrations law students have with writing.

In reality, writing cannot be learned outside of a disciplinary matrix. Legal writing is disciplinary writing, not just another form of technical writing. Law school is a disciplinary community, a discourse community. Within a discourse community, the use of language serves as a point of inclusion or exclusion. Use language as accepted in a discourse community, and you will become credentialed and/or licensed. Fail to familiarize yourself with the

---

2. Mike Rose, *The Language of Exclusion: Writing Instruction and the University*, 47 COLLEGE ENGLISH 341–59, 355 (1985).

disciplinary context of the discourse community, and you will not advance.[3] This book is one small contribution to you, our students, and your efforts to advance.

---

3. David Russell, *Writing Across the Curriculum in Historical Perspective: Toward a Social Interpretation*, 52 COLLEGE ENGLISH 52, 63 (Jan. 1990).

Legal Writing in the Disciplines

Chapter One

A Discipline-Specific Approach to Legal Writing

"A legal writing course must teach first-year law students that they are joining a particular community of legal thinkers and writers. Only in this way will they be able to produce documents that convey the necessary legal analysis effectively to their audience in law practice."[4]

— Jane Kent Gionfriddo

"[W]e must not deny or exaggerate the differences in purpose, audience and context that arise among different disciplines and discourse communities. We must prepare students to expect those differences and to make transitions between different writing situations."[5]

— Jessie C. Grearson

Simply defined, a discipline is a subject that is taught, a field of study, and a branch of learning. Law is all of these things. It is a subject that is taught in various incarnations at the undergraduate level (*i.e.*, *Women, Values and the Law*; *Law and Society*; *The American Legal System*; *The Legal Environment of Business*, etc.). It is a field of study taught in law schools or as examined in sociology and philosophy courses as "The Law." It is also a branch of learning, and a way of seeing, investigating, and understanding the world through a particular lens. Like law, each discipline, whether in the social sciences, sciences, arts, humanities or business, is a way of seeing, investigating, and understanding the world through a particular lens. The particular focus of this text is how writing within the disciplines serves to integrate a student into a disciplinary community, and how disciplinary specific writing is useful in integrating new law students into the discipline of the law.

Law, as a field of study, has the characteristics of any discipline:

---

4. Jane Kent Gionfriddo, *The "Reasonable Zone of Right Answers": Analytical Feedback on Student Writing*, 40 Gonz. L. Rev. 427, 431 n.8 (2005).

5. Jessie C. Grearson, *Teaching the Transitions*, 4 J. Leg. Writing Inst. 57, 58 (1998).

1. Specialized Vocabularies
2. [Writing] Styles
3. Genres
4. Conventions
5. Uses for Texts
6. Intertextual Systems
7. Criteria for Judgment
8. Forums[6]

A student of the law can study it as a system of beliefs expressed as rules and regulations that are enforced and evaluated through institutions. This study of law, "The Law," is often undertaken by sociologists and philosophers, or reserved for upper-level seminars in the law school curriculum. Within "The Law" are specialized areas of study based on subjects that serve as sub-disciplines or legal specializations. The first year law school curriculum is instructive on this point. Most first year law students study the following legal sub-disciplines: Contracts, Property, Torts, Civil Procedure, Criminal Law, and Constitutional Law. Law professors who teach legal writing are most concerned with integrating law students into the legal discipline by teaching the type of writing that legal practitioners do in legal specializations rather than the scholarly writing done in upper division seminars about "The Law" and its sub-disciplines. Legal writing done by practitioners occurs in the context of law as a whole ("The Law") and legal specializations or sub-disciplines.

Let's examine each of the characteristics of law as a discipline in turn.

Specialized Vocabularies

Many new law students have remarked that reading a legal casebook, a type of book used in law classes that contains legal cases on subjects related to the sub-discipline, is like reading a different language. The reason that the people are in court is called a "cause of action." The party bringing the lawsuit becomes the "plaintiff" (short for complaining party), and the party defending against the lawsuit becomes the "defendant." Interspersed with familiar words are Latin words and phrases (*e.g. assumpsit, respondeat superior, replevin, res ipsa loquitor*) that require a legal dictionary to decipher. Additionally, seemingly familiar words become new legal terms of art. For example, the word "serve"

---

6. Charles Bazerman, http://www.education.ucsb.edu/bazerman/chapters/65b.writing disciplines.doc (last visited July 18, 2011).

has a meaning different from its common meaning when used in the phrase "service of process."

Writing Styles

A writing style consists of various strategies that a writer employs when writing about a particular issue and writing to a particular audience. The writing style a legal writer adopts is directly related to the audience they address, whether client, opposing counsel, or court.

Genres

In disciplinary vocabulary, a genre is a type of writing. Case briefs, legal memoranda, client letters, motion briefs, trial briefs, appellate briefs, and opinion letters are all different types of writing that attorneys produce.

Conventions

Conventions are the ways that a writer relates to and/or creates a particular genre. At this point in your education, you are probably familiar with the basic writing conventions for grammar, structure, and usage, as well as the conventions for producing the common genres in your undergraduate or graduate discipline. Each genre of legal writing not only requires the writer to adhere to basic writing conventions (grammar, structure, and usage), but also to genre specific conventions.

Uses for Texts

As used in this book, the word "text" refers to any form of writing. Common legal texts are pieces of factual evidence relevant to a client's case, legal cases (judge made law), statutes (law made by legislatures), regulations (law made by administrative agencies), treatises, law review/journal articles, restatements of the law, and legal periodicals. The basic legal texts that you will use throughout this book are legal cases and statutes. Legal writers use statutes and legal cases to construct client and opinion letters, legal memoranda, and motion, trial, and appellate briefs.

Intertextual Systems

The phrase intertextual systems describes the way that texts relate to each other, their relevance to each other, and their use in the context of each other. At a microscopic level, legal cases are connected to legal memoranda through the synthesis of the rules in the cases and the relationship of that synthesis to the lawyer's analysis of the facts of their client's case. At a macroscopic level, the forums that use and hear the arguments of the parties (law offices, administrative courts, trial courts, and appellate courts) often determine how legal texts relate to each other.

In a law office, a senior attorney may give a new attorney, or associate, an assignment to draft a legal memorandum (legal memo). A legal memo is a document used to communicate an attorney's analysis of a client's case using the appropriate legal texts as authorities, primarily legal cases and statutes. To complete this task, the associate must first determine what area of law is implicated by the facts of the client's case; pull the subject specific cases and/or statutes from a legal research database; critically read those legal authorities; create case briefs (a type of note) for those legal authorities; develop more highly specialized notes on the relationship between the legal authorities and the facts of client's case; make a plan for communicating their analysis of the case; and finally, draft the analysis using the conventions necessary for drafting legal memoranda. While this process is fundamental for drafting legal memoranda, motion, trial, and appellate briefs, and client and opinion letters, the relationship between the texts which utilize the information is determined by the forum itself, specifically, the law office.

For example, the senior attorney may want to use the associate's memorandum to prepare for a meeting with a client or to strategize about what next steps to take in the case. The senior attorney may also want to use the memorandum as a basis to draft a motion brief, a document that communicates arguments to a court and opposing counsel on the client's behalf, to file with the court in a particular dispute. Regardless, the purpose of each and the forum in which they are used determine the relationship between the various legal texts employed.

A Note on the United States Court System as a Forum for Intertextual Systems

In the United States Court System, there are four main types of forums where parties bring their disputes: Administrative Courts (court systems within agencies), State Courts, Tribal Courts (Native American courts), and Federal Courts. Administrative Courts, State Courts, and Federal Courts all have trial courts, appellate courts, and courts of last resort (also known as supreme courts). Because Native American tribes are considered sovereigns and treated as separate nations, *vis-à-vis* the United States, they have their own trial, appellate, and supreme courts.

Agencies, like a state workers' compensation or unemployment benefits division, have their own in-house court system. Each agency has its own separate system to hear arguments and review evidence at the trial court and appellate court levels. Parties who are dissatisfied with an agency decision at the highest level in-agency court may file an appeal with the state trial court. With respect to an agency, a trial court sits as a court of appeals, discussed in more detail below.

Trial courts are the most familiar types of courts. The federal government and each state have trial courts, as do Native American tribes. Federal trial courts are called "District Courts." Trial courts are the courts that you see portrayed on popular law-related television shows and law-related movies. At the trial court level, a single judge hears the arguments from the parties involved in a dispute. A judge or jury may render a decision. If any of the parties are not satisfied with the judge or jury's decision, then they may file an appeal to have the case heard by a higher court.

At the trial court level, the facts of the client's case, as presented through witnesses and pieces of evidence, are analyzed using legal standards that a judge gives as instructions to a jury. Although the same basic types of information are used in this forum as in the law office, the process of the administrative hearing or trial dictates how the legal texts used relate to one another. For example, rules governing trial require the jury to learn the facts of a case through witness testimony and pieces of evidence. The jury learns of the law through instructions given by the judge. Because jurors are not usually legal experts on the cases they hear, lawyers place a premium on relating the various texts used at trial (evidence and testimony) in such a way that creates a cohesive story for the jury, which makes their legal decision seem like common sense. Again, the forum controls the relationship between the texts.

The Federal Government, each state, and some Native American tribes have an appellate court system. The Federal Appellate Court system is perhaps the most complex, as it is divided into units called circuits with an appellate court in each circuit. At the appellate court level, a panel of judges hears the parties seeking and resisting appeal of a trial court's decision. The role of the appellate court is not to rehash what happened at the trial court level. Rather, the court will only hear arguments about an error that the trial court made in deciding the case before it. Appellate judges hear no new witnesses or evidence, but are limited to the record of what transpired in the trial court. Accordingly, the lawyer presenting a case before an appellate court is limited in which texts they can use and how they can be used. For example, in the appellate brief, the lawyer can only discuss the relationship between the legal authorities to the extent that they have direct bearing on the error alleged on appeal. Similarly, the only facts available to the attorney in an appellate proceeding are those contained in the record.

Supreme Courts are a type of appellate court. They function the same way as the appellate courts described above with two key distinctions: Supreme Courts have the ability to select the cases that they will hear and they are also more powerful than standard appellate courts, in that they are charged with the responsibility of interpreting the Constitution of the United States (United States Supreme Court) or the state constitution (state supreme courts in any of the 50 states). A party who wishes a Supreme Court, or court of last resort, to hear a case must file an application to the court. This application is called a *writ of certiorari.*

Consider the diagrams on the facing page. When creating legal documents to bring in a particular forum, a lawyer is bound by the law of that forum. For example, if a lawyer is litigating a case in a state trial court they are bound by the law of that particular state. If a lawyer is litigating a case in a federal court, then they are bound by the federal law of the circuit which includes that particular state. The law that the lawyer must apply from a particular forum is called "mandatory authority."

In cases where the law in a forum is silent about the issues raised in a client's case, a lawyer is permitted to use the law in another forum when creating legal documents. The law that a lawyer is permitted to use is called "persuasive authority." When a court has not heard an issue that a client's case raises, this issue is called an "issue of first impression." A court may be persuaded by the law from other forums to help it decide how to rule in such a case.

Criteria for Judgment

Law, like every other discipline, has criteria for judging pieces of writing. Case briefs, legal memoranda, and motion, trial, and appellate briefs, all genres of legal writing, are evaluated on whether the writing accomplishes the overall purpose of the genre as well as each of its distinct parts. The purpose of a piece of writing, the reason for its creation, is called its "rhetorical purpose".

Forums

All disciplines have forums or places where its scholars share their written contributions to the discipline with other scholars (journals) and get together in person to discuss the field, scholarship, and other matters related to the profession (conferences). A law professor primarily publishes in a law review,

Diagram of Court Hierarchies in the American Legal System

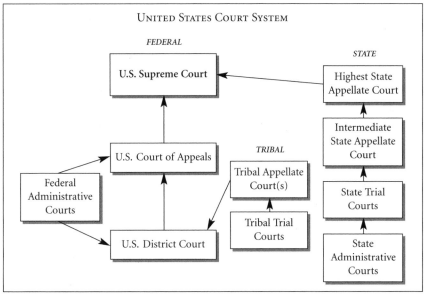

(Diagram created by Robert Clinton)

U.S. Court of Appeals and District Court Map

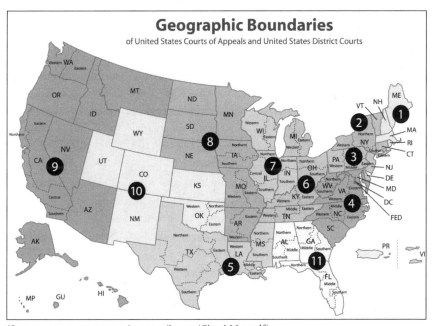

(Source—www.uscourts.gov/uscourts/images/CircuitMap.pdf)

a type of law journal, and attends conferences on "The Law," topics related to their area of legal specialization, and on issues in the legal academy (legal education). In contrast, practicing attorneys create written documents on behalf of clients, which are filed in a court. Many of these documents go on to form the basis for published legal cases, which serve as the criteria for evaluating subsequent disputes before the court in the same or similar legal and factual areas. Like law professors, lawyers attend conferences. However, these conferences are usually in the form of continuing legal education seminars (CLEs). These seminars contain information about legal specializations as they relate to practicing law, not the scholarly study of law. Lawyers must attend a certain number of CLEs each year to maintain their license to practice law.

EXERCISE 1: Take a moment to consider your undergraduate and/or graduate discipline. List the specialized vocabulary, writing styles, genres, conventions, uses for texts, intertextual systems, criteria for judgment, and forums for your discipline.

How to Use This Book

This book is a book of translation. Its purpose is to translate the foundational concepts of legal analysis and writing into the language of the discipline most familiar to you. Each section in Chapter One has a corresponding section in Chapters Two–Six. For example, Chapter One, Section 1-1 corresponds to Sections 2-1, 3-1, 4-1, 5-1, and 6-1 in Chapters Two–Six. To get the most out of each concept in this text, first read a section in Chapter One and then its counterpart in the chapter with the perspective from the discipline most familiar to you.

Each chapter contains numerous annotated examples, as well as opportunities for you to complete exercises and self-check your work with model answers to those exercises. The examples, exercises, and exercise answers for each chapter are located on the CD-ROM accompanying this text. A complete listing of the examples and exercises for each chapter is located at the end of the chapter. A complete listing of model answers is located at the end of the book. By reviewing the examples and completing the exercises provided, you will more quickly and efficiently assimilate the foundational skills necessary for effective legal analysis and writing.

Section 1-1: The Legal Memo — Legal Writing to Inform

The legal memo is a common genre of writing done by attorneys. Its rhetorical purpose is to inform an attorney about possible arguments for and against a client in a particular matter, to explain possible outcomes for a client's case, and to alert others working on a case to any unknown information that must be gathered and any other actions that must be taken on the case. Other attorneys at the author's workplace are the intended audience for the memo. Usually, memos are not filed with the court or shared with attorneys outside of the author's workplace.

In a legal memo, an attorney communicates in writing an analysis of the facts of the client's case using a synthesis of relevant legal authorities as an analytical framework. The attorney can communicate the analysis via e-mail or in a formal printed memo. Regardless of the means an attorney uses to communicate her analysis, the basic parts of a legal memo and the rhetorical purpose of each part are the same. These parts are illustrated in the chart on the next page.

MATERIALS: A template of the standard memo structure is in the Legal Memo Case File folder located in the Exercises & Materials for this chapter.

To construct a legal memo, a legal writer takes the following steps: (1) determines what area of law is implicated by the facts of the client's case; (2) locates and gathers the subject specific cases and/or statutes from a legal research database; (3) critically reads those legal authorities; (4) creates case briefs (a type of note) for those legal authorities; (5) develops more highly specialized notes on the relationship between the legal authorities and the facts of the client's case; (6) makes a plan for communicating their analysis of the case; (7) drafts the analysis using the conventions necessary for drafting legal memoranda (see table above); and (8) explains in a conclusion the most likely outcome to the client's case. This portion of the chapter will discuss steps 1 and 3–8 in turn. Because you have been given a case file with legal authorities to work from in constructing the legal memo, this book will not discuss the legal research process.

Basic Parts of a Legal Memo and the Rhetorical Purpose of Each Part

Parts of the Memo	Rhetorical Purpose
"To, From, Date, Re" Caption	Communicates the intended recipient of the memo, the person who drafted it, the date it was drafted, and the matter it regards.
Issue(s), also known as Question(s) Presented	Framed as a "yes" or "no" question. Communicates to the reader: 1. The area or areas of law that the case involves; 2. The particular legal question that the memo seeks to answer; and 3. The facts of the client's case that are important to resolving that question. The Issue/QP also functions as the main idea of the memo. It describes the purpose for which it was written.
Short Answer(s), also known as Brief Answer(s)	A miniature version of the conclusion that: 1. Sets out a "yes or no" (or probably yes or no) answer to the Question(s) Presented; 2. States the legal standard for evaluating the facts; and 3. Then briefly describes how the facts of the client's case meet or do not meet the legal standard.
Statement of Facts	Objectively communicates the salient facts of the client's case to the reader by summary, paraphrase, and quotation. The facts are not skewed in favor of the client but presented in a fair and unbiased manner.
Discussion	The section of the memo where the attorney communicates their analysis of the client's case. Prior to communicating the analysis, the attorney gives a brief overview of the requirements for the cause of action. If the cause of action is statutory, then the attorney sets forth the relevant statutory language and explains it briefly. In communicating the analysis the attorney: 1. Sets forth the framework for analyzing the facts of the client's case (the synthesis of legal authorities) first; and 2. Then uses that framework to analyze the facts of the client's case (factual analysis). All of the facts included in this section must be included in the *Statement of Facts*. The attorney sets forth the synthesis of legal authorities and then the factual analysis for each of the legal issue
Conclusion	Communicates the most likely outcome to the client's case. In some instances also contains a checklist of next actions to take on the case.

Section 1-2: Reading and Note-taking Strategies for Legal Authorities

Reading

A text is an object that an author deliberately builds. It is constructed of parts ordered in a certain manner for a specified purpose. You have to disassemble those parts and reassemble them for your purposes. However, in order to do this you have to understand how the text is constructed.[7] Before reading any legal text (case book, statutes, cases, memo, brief, etc.), ask yourself the following questions:

Why type of text is it?

Why was it written?

How do I find information within it?

How can I use the material in it for a particular purpose?[8]

Statutes and Cases

Statutes

Statutes and cases are the most common types of texts from which lawyers gather the rules that function as the framework for analyzing the facts in a client's case. Both are often referred to as "legal authorities." A statute is a rule or group of rules made by legislators located in a book called a "code." As you read through a statute, you will notice immediately the name of the state where the legislature created the statute and information about the location of the statute in its print or electronic form. Next, you will encounter the body of the statute. In order to understand it, you must first determine the rule or rule it contains, break the rule into its component parts to determine what each part means, and then re-assemble the parts of the statute to determine what each part means in the context of the entire body. Understanding the basic rules of grammar and punctuation is essential to this process. Periods contain different meanings than commas and semi-colons, and the use of any of these forms of punctuation can change the meaning of subsequent sections of the statute in context. In determining what a statute means comprehensively, lawyers familiarize themselves with the literal meaning of the words and punctuation in it. Additionally, the statute may refer to other portions of the code

---

7. MARK HJORTSHOJ, THE TRANSITION TO COLLEGE WRITING 130 (2001).
8. *Id.* at 128.

where it is located or may contain words that are explained in the definitions section of the code.

MATERIALS: Examples of a statute, *"Dyeing or selling dyed baby fowl or rabbits,"* and statutory diagram for it are in the Reading and Note-taking folder located in the Exercises & Materials for this chapter.

EXERCISE 2: Diagram the statute for this Exercise to (1) determine the rule or rules that it contains; (2) break the rule into its parts to determine what each part means; and (3) re-assemble the parts to determine what each part of the statute means in the context of the entire body. Do not neglect to read the statute closely to ascertain the use of grammar and the meaning of its punctuation.

MATERIALS: The statute for Exercise 2, *"Unlawful bear exploitation,"* is in the Reading and Note-taking folder located in the Exercises & Materials for this chapter.

Because statues are written to cover a broad range of conduct, the words used in them are often subject to multiple meanings. For example, a criminal statute may enhance the penalty for a crime if the perpetrator of the crime uses a "dangerous weapon." The word "dangerous" in this context could have multiple meanings. If the definition section of the statute does not define the word "dangerous," or the definition is unclear, then a lawyer would next conduct research to determine if any cases define the words in the statute. For the most part, cases define, clarify, and interpret statutes. They also utilize the guidelines legislators use to construct statutes, the "cannons of construction," to aid in interpreting the statute.

Cases

Our judicial system operates on the doctrine of *stare decisis* or the doctrine of precedent. Essentially, the doctrine of precedent requires a court to make consistent decisions in resolving legal problems involving similar factual situations. A case, a type of legal authority, is a written record of a court's resolution of a particular legal problem or issue. It is a written opinion by an appellate court concerning an error made by a trial court in deciding a particular legal issue. Lawyers study cases to determine how a court will likely resolve the legal issue the lawyer has been asked to resolve. Information in cases usually proceeds in the following order:

1. At the top of the first page of the case is the legal citation. The citation gives information to the reader about how to find the case. A case citation begins with the number of the volume of the book where the case can be found. These books are called reporters. Next in the legal citation is an abbreviation for the name of the book. The last part of the case citation is a number indicating the first page on which the case begins. All of this information precedes the actual legal opinion, as does a caption containing the name of the court rendering the opinion, the names of the parties to the lawsuit, and the date that the opinion was rendered.

2. At the start of the opinion, the appellate judge writing the opinion briefly states the legal path the case took to arrive at the appellate court. For example, the judge will state why the case went to trial, the legal issues that the trier of fact (the judge or the jury) was asked to decide at trial, the outcome at trial, the error that the appellate court (the court at the next level) was asked to review, and a brief synopsis of what the appellate court decided.

3. Next, a case will either proceed with the legal issue the appellate court is asked to review or a brief statement of the facts introduced at the trial court level. This information is given as context for the court's identification of the relevant law that it will apply to resolve the issues in the case.

4. After the judge has stated or implied the legal issue for review and given the reader sufficient facts for context, he or she will first state the lens through which the appellate court is reviewing the case (the standard of review) and then develop a legal rule from other cases that resolved similar issues. The judge will assemble a rule for use in his or her case by (1) categorizing the legal problem before the court; (2) choosing cases from the same category; and (3) discussing the concepts from those cases that have direct bearing on the outcome of the case before it in a logical and organized manner. In this discussion, the judge will explain the pivotal facts in those cases and how they shaped the legal outcome. The judge will also use factual illustrations from the case law that are similar to the case before the court in explaining the legal concepts. This process is known as "rule synthesis" or "synthesis of legal authorities."

5. Once the judge has developed the rule that will help resolve the legal issue in the case before the court, the judge uses the rule synthesis as a framework for the purpose of analyzing the facts of the case. In analyzing the facts, the judge (1) categorizes the facts in the manner they were categorized in the rule synthesis cases, using only those facts that the case law suggests are relevant; (2) compares how the facts in the

case before it are like or unlike the facts in the applicable case law; (3) explains the relationships between those comparisons using the language from the rule synthesis; and (4) connects all of the explanations moving from point to point, assertion to assertion, until all of the possible plausible explanations are exhausted. This process is known as "legal (factual) analysis."

6. Lastly, the judge drafts a conclusion stating how the court has decided the case based on the analysis.

   The opinion of the judge in the final disposition of the case is known as the "majority opinion."

7. If the other judges on the appellate panel disagree with the reasoning in the majority opinion but not the final outcome of the case, then a judge or group of judges will draft what is known as a "concurring opinion." In writing that concurring opinion, a judge will either use the synthesis of authorities as articulated in the majority opinion but ascribe a different meaning to it in analyzing the facts or develop a new synthesis of authorities that emphasizes different areas of the law and use it to analyze the facts.

8. If the other judges on the appellate panel disagree with the reasoning in the majority opinion as well as the outcome of the case, then a judge or group of judges will draft what is known as a "dissenting opinion." In drafting a dissenting opinion, the judges will usually either use the synthesis of legal authorities in the majority opinion and apply it to the facts for a different outcome or re-develop the synthesis of authorities and apply it to the facts for a different outcome.

In older judicial opinions, all of these pieces are usually present. However, they may not appear in this order.

A lawyer or judge would also use the process above to determine the meaning of a statute (a written law made by a legislature) and its application to the case before it. Cases define statutes; so in creating its synthesis of legal authorities, the court would examine the cases that provided definitions for the key parts of the statute at issue. Lastly, a lawyer or judge would also use the process above in conducting a purely legal analysis that was not based on the facts of a client's case but the meaning of the law. In such an instance, the law at issue would be treated just like the facts of the case but analyzed using the applicable legal standard.

MATERIALS: An example of a case, "*Stambovsky v. Ackley (crd)*," labeled in this manner is in the Reading and Note-taking folder located in the Exercises & Materials for this chapter.

EXERCISE 3: Now that you know what to expect when you read a case, please read all of the cases in the Legal Memo Case File in chronological order and then label them with the parts set forth above. The Legal Memo Case File is located in the Exercises & Materials for this chapter. After you have finished reading and labeling the cases, read the assigning memo in the case file and the documents listed there.

Note-taking

A case brief is a type of note that lawyers take on the cases that they read. Its rhetorical purpose is to provide a map of the case in shorthand form. The parts of a case, as expressed in the case brief, are mimicked in almost every form of legal writing. The following tables illustrate how the parts of a case brief correspond to the parts of a legal memo and show the structure and purpose of the parts of a case brief.

Corresponding Parts of a Case/Case Brief and Legal Memo

Parts of a Case/Case Brief	Parts of a Legal Memo
Case Name and Citation	"To, From, Date, Re" Caption
Procedural Posture	*Usually contained in the Statement of Facts*
Issue(s)	Question(s) Presented
Facts	Statement of Facts
Ratio Decidendi (RD): *Synthesis of Legal Authorities and Factual Analysis*	Discussion Section: *Synthesis of Legal Authorities, Factual Analysis*
Ruling	Short Answer(s); Conclusion
Holding	Short Answer(s); Conclusion

MATERIALS: An example of a standard case brief template for legal writing, a case brief for *Stambovsky v. Ackley*, and a copy of *Stambovsky v. Ackley* labeled with the parts of a case brief and memo are in the Reading and Note-taking folder in the Exercises & Materials for this chapter.

Parts of a Case/Case Brief and the Rhetorical Purpose of Each

Parts of a Case/ Case Brief	Rhetorical Purpose
Case Name and Citation	Contains the names of a case (the parties to the lawsuit) and a citation to the actual case reporter (print or electronic copy) where the case may be found. The citation begins with a number (the volume of the book where the case may be found), proceeds with an abbreviation for the case reporter (the actual book where the case may be found), and ends with another number (the first page on which the case begins).
Procedural Posture	A brief synopsis of the path that case took to arrive at the appellate court issuing the opinion. Also contains the legal decision rendered by the court or courts below that heard the case previously.
Facts	Communicates the salient facts of the client's case to the reader by summary, paraphrase, and quotation.
Issue(s)	In a case, this section communicates to the reader the legal question before the court. In a case brief, this section should communicate to the reader: 1. The area or areas of law that the case involves; 2. The particular legal question that the memo seeks to answer; and 3. The facts of the client's case that are important to resolving that question.
Ratio Decidendi (RD) —Literally "the reason or rationale for the decision."	This is the section of the case where the judge communicates his or her analysis of the case before the court, and the part of the case brief where the legal writer articulates the court's reasoning in their own words. This portion of the case brief should explain: 1. The legal framework that the court used to analyze the facts before it (synthesis of legal authorities); and 2. How the court used that framework to actually analyze the facts before it (factual analysis).
Ruling	The decision that the judge or judges made in the case about who won and who lost, and what the winning party was awarded.
Holding	The rule that emerges from the case, the proposition for which the case stands, and the implication of the court's decision for future, similar situations.

EXERCISE 4: Using the *Case Brief Template for Legal Writing*, brief all of the cases in the Legal Memo Case File. Prior to briefing, look back over your labeled cases. On a separate piece of paper, list the definitions of any words that you do not know, note any concepts that you do not understand, and jot down any other points of confusion and/or reflection as you move through each part of the case.

Once you know how the most basic building block of legal writing, a case, is constructed you can manipulate the parts in a manner that will allow you to understand the material in a way most comfortable for you. You will need to take notes on the case in preparation for the different types of legal writing that you will do. While the case brief provides you with a good map of the case, it is in no way comprehensive enough to prepare you for the task of writing a legal memo.

The note-taking that you do for a client's case can take a number of forms. Four effective types of notes for legal note-taking are listing, free writing, cubing, and collaborative learning.[9] Our focus is on the first three. Making a list, or listing, is probably the easiest and least fancy way to engage in note-taking. It involves making a list. If you choose this strategy, focus on any emerging patterns with respect to legal principles and facts that you see in the cases that you have read and their relationship to the facts of your client's case.

MATERIALS: An example of listing is in the Model Answers folder for this chapter under Exercise 5.

Free writing is also an option for note-taking. The key is not to restrict any thoughts that pop into your head about the cases you have read and their relationship to your client's case. Do not be concerned with sentence structure or the efficacy of your ideas at this point. Just write.

MATERIALS: An example of free writing is located in the Model Answers folder for this chapter under Exercise 5.

Cubing is an approach to note-taking that is named for the sides of a cube. As a cube has 6 sides, so does the cubing approach have 6 steps that will help you

---

9. Donald A. Daiker, Andrew Kerek & Max Morenburg, The Writer's Options: Combining to Composing 333–334 (3d ed. 1986).

to take notes.[10] Use the following six steps for the cubing approach to taking notes:[11]

1. **Describe the holdings in each of your cases.**

2. **Compare the holdings to one another.** *Starting with the holding from the case earliest in time and progressing to the holding from the case latest in time, explain how the law changes. What new characteristics are added to the holding with each passing case? What characteristics of the holding remain unchanged with each passing case? What characteristics of the holding are ultimately discarded or rendered less significant?*

3. **Associate the body of law that results from the cases.** The body of law consists of all of the holdings, taken together. *What implications do the holdings have for the facts of your client's case?*

4. **List the legal categories and concepts in which your cases fall.**

5. **Group your relevant case facts and the facts that are similar from your client's case with appropriate categories and concepts.**

6. **Generate arguments both for and against your client.** *Based on the legal authorities and the facts of your client's case, what could help your client to win? What could cause your client to lose?*

MATERIALS: An example of cubing is in the Model Answers folder for this chapter under Exercise 5.

Regardless of what form your notes take, they must be thorough enough to aid you in understanding the cases that you read. They must also help you to make connections between the law in the cases and the facts of the client's case for the purpose of resolving the client's legal issue(s). Taking notes on each case that you read will help you to develop a more thorough synthesis of your legal authorities and its implications for your client's case.

EXERCISE 5: Using any of the note-taking methods detailed above, take notes on your client's case.

---

10. *Id.* at 340–342.

11. These concepts are taken from *id.*, but I have modified them to fit a legal writing context. The steps as listed there are as follows: "(1) describe your subject; (2) compare your subject; (3) associate your subject; (4) analyze your subject; (5) apply your subject; and (6) argue for or against your subject."

After you have completed your notes for all of the cases, review them. How has your understanding of the issue become more refined? Can you summarize the key legal principles in each case and how they build upon and relate to each other? What types of facts are important to the court in deciding cases like the ones you have read? You should be able to answer these questions **before** you move on to organizing and synthesizing your legal authorities.

EXERCISE 6: After answering the questions in the previous paragraph, create a Question or Question(s) Presented for the memo you will write on your client's case. You may revise the QP(s) as you organize and synthesize your legal authorities.

MATERIALS: Directions for drafting Questions Presented are in the Legal Memo Case File folder located in the Exercises & Materials for this chapter.

Section 1-3: Organizing and Synthesizing Legal Authorities

Organization

When synthesizing legal authorities, a lawyer's or court's goal is to find patterns in facts and in the reasoning used to resolve the issues raised by various factual scenarios. The resolution of these issues is memorialized in cases. After the author has closely read the cases for patterns, they then integrate the cases based on those patterns into a seamless piece of writing. In gathering cases for a synthesis of authorities, you should select cases that have facts similar to the facts in your case, as well as cases that clarify your understanding of the court's reasoning used to resolve the issues raised by the factual scenario before it. The legal authorities in your *Legal Memo Case File* have been selected for you in accordance with these guidelines.

Before you begin synthesizing your legal authorities, review your case briefs and notes from the previous section. After you have completed this task, you must *determine* the cause of action (the legal area that the case involves), *categorize* the cases by issue, and then *define* the category and its concepts (pulling the rules and analysis out of the cases). You can most effectively complete these three steps by organizing the material using the strategies that follow. Do not neglect to organize; failure to do so will result in an unfocused synthesis and, ultimately, an unfocused and poorly constructed memo.

The organization for any piece of writing depends on the overall purpose of the writing. Remember, the rhetorical purpose of a synthesis of legal authorities (or rule synthesis) is to provide a framework for analyzing the facts of your client's case. In constructing your synthesis, you will need to sort the cases by cause of action, next by category or the particular issues they explore, and finally, by the concepts that the court elaborates on within each category. You can accomplish these tasks by organizing the information in an outline or a MindMap. An outline is an organizational structure that follows the basic structure of your synthesis and gives a brief description of the content as arranged in each section. A MindMap accomplishes the same goal as an outline, but does so in a less linear fashion.

MATERIALS: Samples of an outline and MindMap are in the Model
Answers folder for this chapter under Exercise 7.

EXERCISE 7: Using your case briefs and notes from the previous section, arrange them in either an outline or a MindMap.

Synthesis

Now that you have organized the information in your case file, you are ready to draft your synthesis of legal authorities for your memo. The synthesis is the first part of your memo *Discussion* section. In drafting a synthesis of the relevant legal authorities, you must do the following:

Determine the cause of action. *What area or areas of law does the cause of action involve?*

Categorize the authorities according to the questions that you want answered OR issues that you want to explore within the cause of action.

Define the category and its concepts. Legal categories are determined both by the cause of action and the legal issues the court endeavors to solve. Legal concepts are the set of ideas or approaches that a court sets as the criteria for resolving the parts of a legal issue. For example, in a case where someone tripped over an object in a grocery store aisle, they would bring a cause of action for negligence. Negligence is the cause of action, or broad legal category, under which the case falls. In the category of negligence are several concepts or elements that the court uses to approach a negligence claim. For every allegation of negligence, the court determines whether the party accused of negligence had a duty to the injured party, whether the duty was breached, and whether the breach of the duty was the cause of the injury. In sum, the concepts or set of approaches for a negligence claim are duty, breach, causation, and harm. This same set of approaches also serves as categories for the concepts or elements within them. For example, if a claim concerns only whether a duty was owed to the injury party, then the court will determine the set of approaches it will use to resolve this question. Ultimately, the number and layers of categories and concepts is dependent upon the legal cause of action.

<u>Compare</u> and <u>Contrast</u> similarities and differences between the authorities using the major concepts from the authorities, organized by category.

<u>Explain</u> those similarities and differences in turn and how they impact your understanding of the relationship between authorities for the major concepts in each category.

<u>Understand</u> how those similarities and differences alter your reading of subsequent authorities.

<u>Connect</u> all of your explanations moving from concept to concept, category to category, until you have exhausted all of your available relevant authority (primarily case law). In explaining the concepts, you may want to use factual illustrations from the cases if they aid in those explanations. If you do include factual illustrations, make sure that you organize them after a cohesive discussion of the relevant legal authorities. You want to make sure that the reader has a grasp on the resulting authority from the court's reasoning process before you use facts to illustrate conceptual threads within those authorities.

When a court or lawyer synthesizes legal authorities objectively, they establish the boundaries for a cause of action. In issuing an opinion (which contains an objective synthesis of authorities), the court decides to do one of three things: (1) to expand the legal category to include the added characteristics that the new case brings to its concepts; (2) constrict the legal category to exclude the added characteristics that the new case brings to its concepts; or (3) maintain its existing boundaries for the legal category and its concepts and evaluate the case within those boundaries.

As you are synthesizing your rules objectively, answer the following questions for each case:

1. *In formulating its rule, has the court expanded the legal categories and concepts that are relevant to resolving the lawsuit? If it has, then what characteristics from the case before it did it add to the categories and concepts?*

2. *In formulating its rule, has the court constricted the legal categories and concepts that are relevant to resolving the lawsuit? If it did, then what characteristics from the case before it did it exclude from the categories and concepts?*

3. *In formulating its rule, has the court maintained the boundaries for the legal categories and its concepts that are relevant to resolving the lawsuit? If it did, then how is the category defined? What are the boundaries for the categories and concepts?*

A Brief Note about Citation and Citation Form

Just like writers in any other discipline, legal writers give attribution to the authorities that they use in constructing a piece of writing. In writing a synthesis of legal authorities, a legal writer will cite to the case or statute from which they are paraphrasing, summarizing, or quoting by using a proper citation format. The two types of legal citation forms taught in law school are based on two books: *The Bluebook: A Uniform System of Citation*; and the *ALWD Citation Manual: A Professional System of Citation*. If you are in law school, you will learn how to give proper attribution based on either of these books. If you are using this book as an undergraduate enrolled in a pre-law program, please use the citation form appropriate for your particular discipline.

EXERCISE 8: Using your outline or MindMap, draft a synthesis of legal authorities for the *Discussion* section of your memo. Make sure that you use the techniques outlined above. Do not forget to give proper attribution to your legal authorities.

Section 1-4: Using Legal Authorities to Analyze Facts and to Develop Conclusions

Analysis

When a lawyer analyzes the facts of a case, they use the synthesis of legal authorities as the sole criterion by which to evaluate the strengths and weakness of the case and to predict how a court is likely to rule on the case. The lawyer uses the synthesis as the basis for the reasoning in the analysis to resolve the relevant legal issues. Courts and lawyers use two types of reasoning: inductive reasoning (an assertion concluding how the court should decide this issue followed by reasons for that conclusion) or deductive reasoning (reasons leading to an assertion concluding how the court should decide this issue). Prior to analyzing the facts of a case, you must make sure that you have thoroughly synthesized your legal authorities by defining and explaining their categories and concepts in a cohesive, seamless and complete manner. An incomplete synthesis of authorities will lead to an incomplete factual analysis.

When a court or a lawyer analyzes facts objectively, they further reinforce the boundaries that the court has set for the cause of action by determining which facts and reasoning have relevance in resolving the legal issue(s) within those boundaries. In analyzing the facts of each case, a court or lawyer decides whether the facts of the case before it and the reasoning used to resolve issues involving those facts are relevant and/or included within the scope of the boundaries previously set for the cause of action by doing any of the following: (1) comparing the facts in the case to similar facts in the precedent authorities to explain why the outcome in the precedent authority and the reasoning used to create that authority should be applied; (2) contrasting the facts in the case to dissimilar facts in the precedent authorities in order to explain why the outcome in the precedent authority and the reasoning used to create that authority should not be applied; and (3) comparing and contrasting the similarities and differences between the facts in the case and the facts in the precedent authority to explain why the outcome in the precedent authority and the reasoning used to create that authority should be applied to include the facts of the case before it despite the difference in the facts.

Before beginning a draft of your objective analysis, you should review the facts of the cases as set out in your case briefs, the reasoning the court used in resolving the issue(s) raised by the facts, and your notes on the cases.

As you are reviewing your case briefs and notes, you should ask yourself the following questions:

1. *Are the facts of my client's case similar to the facts in the relevant legal authorities? If so, how are they same? Given the similarities in the facts and the applicable reasoning in the legal authorities, what is the likely outcome of my client's case?*

2. *Are the facts of my client's case different from the facts in the relevant legal authorities? If so, how are they different? How do the differences in the case facts alter the likely outcome of my client's case given the applicable reasoning in the authorities?*

3. *If the facts in my client's case are different from the facts in the relevant legal authorities, are there any reasons why precedent authority should control the outcome of my client's case?*

In drafting your analysis of the facts in your client's case, you must do the following:

1. <u>Categorize</u> the facts under the same categories you used in your synthesis of authorities based on the issue for which they are relevant. You will accomplish this in your analysis by simply following the organizational structure that you created in your synthesis of authorities. Where your synthesis for a particular concept within a particular category ends, you should begin your analysis. As you begin your analysis, you will need to make a decision about whether you will use inductive reasoning (an assertion concluding how the court should decide this issue followed by reasons) or deductive reasoning (reasons leading to an assertion concluding how the court should decide this issue) for your analysis. This choice will influence how you draft your topic sentences for each category and concept that you analyze.

2. <u>Compare</u> and <u>Contrast</u> the facts in the case with the facts in the legal authorities starting with facts that are relevant for the first category and concept, and then taking each subsequent category and concept in turn. Do not start your analysis of one concept and category before finishing your analysis of another. Be sure to complete numbers 2–5 for each category and concept.

3. <u>Explain</u> the relationships between those comparisons using the language from the synthesis of authorities. How do the facts meet the criteria set out in the synthesis of authorities? How do the facts not meet the criteria set out in the synthesis of authorities?

4. <u>Connect</u> all of the explanations moving from point to point, assertion to assertion, until all of the plausible explanations are exhausted FOR AND AGAINST YOUR SIDE. Be sure to complete your analysis of a concept (the explanations for your side) before moving on to the counter-analysis (the explanations against your side).

5. <u>Conclude</u> based on the weight of your analysis. This is a one to three sentence conclusion at the end of each concept, not the longer conclusion that will appear at the end of your memo.

A Brief Note about Citation and Citation Form

Just like writers in any other discipline, legal writers give attribution to the authorities that they use in constructing a piece of writing. In writing a factual analysis, a legal writer will cite to the documents in the case file or an official record of the proceeding from which they are paraphrasing, summarizing or quoting using a proper citation format. Both the *Bluebook* and the *ALWD Manual* cover citation to documents and the record. If you are in law school, you will learn how to give proper attribution based on either of these books. If you are using this text as an undergraduate enrolled in a pre-law program, please use the citation form appropriate for your particular discipline.

EXERCISE 9: Using the objective rule synthesis that you drafted for your legal memo as the sole criterion for evaluation, draft an objective factual analysis using the facts in your client's case. Do not forget to give attribution to your legal and factual authorities.

Drafting the Statement of Facts

The *Statement of Facts* for your legal memo must be objective. Your goal in drafting it is to inform your audience about what happened in the case. The *Statement of Facts* for a legal memo should not be slanted toward any particular point of view but rather should present the facts in a fair and straightforward manner. The organizational structure should support the best telling of the story. Do not forget to provide attribution for the facts throughout this section where necessary. All of the facts that appear in your analysis must appear in your *Statement of Facts*.

EXERCISE 10: Using the facts presented in your case file, draft an objective *Statement of Facts*.

Developing Conclusions

The purpose of the *Conclusion* section of the memo is for you to communicate the most plausible outcome of your client's case. This section is also used to alert the memo recipient of any information that is unknown about the client's case and needed to resolve the client's legal issue, and/or any next steps that must be taken on the client's behalf.

The *Short Answer(s)* located at the beginning of the memo is a miniature version of the *Conclusion*. In it, the writer answers the *Question(s) Presented*.

MATERIALS: Directions for drafting Short Answers are in the Memo Case File folder located in the Exercises & Materials for this chapter.

PUTTING IT ALL TOGETHER:
Using the skills that you have learned for constructing a legal memo, complete the legal memo assignment for the case file assigned to you.

Section 1-5: The Legal Brief— Legal Writing to Persuade

The legal brief is a genre of writing used primarily by trial lawyers or litigators. Its rhetorical purpose is twofold: to tell the client's legal story using a plausible theory that explains the client's conduct resulting in the cause of action; and to provide arguments to persuade a judge to adopt that theory and any proposed outcomes for the case. The intended audiences for the legal brief are the judge and opposing counsel. Many briefs are filed in support of motions or applications to the court requesting that the court either take or prevent an action. Motions are governed by a standard of review, a set of legal rules setting out the requirements that must be met to prevail using a particular motion.

In a legal brief, the attorney communicates in writing a persuasive analysis of the facts of the client's case, also known as "arguments," using a carefully crafted persuasive synthesis of the relevant legal authorities as an analytical framework. The attorney's arguments are presented in written and/or electronic form over the various parts that constitute the brief. Each part of the brief serves its overall rhetorical purpose: to persuade. The parts of a legal brief and their purposes are set out in the chart on the next page. Each of these parts will not be found in every brief, but they represent the basic components of legal briefs.

MATERIALS: A template of the standard structure for a legal brief is in the Legal Brief Case File folder located in the Exercises & Materials for this chapter.

To construct a legal brief, the writer must complete the same steps used to complete a legal memo, with several modifications. To review, a lawyer must complete the following steps to draft a legal brief: (1) determine what area of law is implicated by the facts of the client's case; (2) locate and gather the subject-specific cases and/or statutes from a legal research database; (3) critically read those legal authorities; (4) create case briefs (a type of note) for those legal authorities; (5) develop more highly specialized notes on the relationship between the legal authorities and the facts of the client's case; (6) develop a plausible theory for the client conduct that resulted in the cause of action; (7) make a plan for communicating the arguments that support the theory of the case; and (8) draft those arguments using the conventions necessary for drafting legal briefs.

Even if the brief is on the same material covered by a memo, the writer must review the cases and any additional cases that have subsequently become relevant, update the case briefs and notes, develop a theory of the case, make a plan for communicating arguments that support the theory of the case, and draft the brief. In the remainder of the chapter, we will revisit steps 1 and 3–8 as they relate to the legal brief. Because you have been given a case file with legal authorities to work from in constructing the legal memo and brief, this book will not discuss the research process.

Reading and Note-taking

Reading

The process of reading for the purpose of creating a legal brief is basically the same as for creating a legal memo. One slight change is that for the legal

Basic Parts of a Legal Brief and the Rhetorical Purpose of Each Part

Parts of a Legal Brief	Rhetorical Purpose
Notice of Motion or Cover Sheet	Gives notice to the party defending against a cause of action that a motion and/or brief supporting the motion have been filed by opposing counsel (notice of motion). The party responding to the motion uses a cover sheet. Both contain the case caption, case number assigned by the court, and a host of other information as required by the jurisdiction (forum) in which the motion is brought.
Certificate of Service	Certifies that a copy of the brief has been filed with the appropriate court and that a copy has been sent to opposing counsel.
Table of Contents	Provides the reader with an overview of the arguments contained in the brief as communicated through the point headings. Point headings are persuasively written subject headings for each part of the argument in the brief.
Table of Authorities (*mostly present in longer legal briefs*)	Communicates the type and weight of legal authority that the brief writer used to support the legal arguments in the brief.
Motion Standard of Review	Sets the requirements for a party to prevail using a particular motion through a case or group of synthesized cases.
Introduction	Introduces the reader to the theory of the case (the theme or main idea for the entire brief) through a summary of the attorney's best persuasive arguments as found in the brief. It also sets out the procedural posture of the case.
Statement of Facts	Persuasively communicates the salient facts of the client's case to the reader by summary, paraphrase, and quotation. The writer re-tells the facts of the case through the client's eyes in a manner that supports the theory of the case.
Argument	Communicates the attorney's persuasive factual analysis or arguments made on the client's behalf. Carefully explains the reasoning as developed across cases (persuasive synthesis of legal authorities) in a manner that supports the theory of the case. Uses that synthesis as the framework to build arguments (factual analysis) on behalf of the client. All of the facts used in this section must be included in the *Statement of Facts*.
Conclusion (Prayer for Relief)	Formally requests from the court the relief or preferred outcome to the case.

brief the legal reader must pay close attention to the patterns of reasoning that the court adopts across cases and the range of facts included in that reasoning. Critical legal readers employ the same process in reading cases for the legal memo. However, the legal brief requires the writer to take the additional step of reading the legal authorities to develop a plausible explanation or explanations for the client conduct that created the cause of action. This explanation for why a client conducted himself or herself in such a way as to land in court is called the "theory of the case." The theory of the case is the main theme that pervades every part of the legal brief.

Note-taking

The note-taking process for the legal brief includes all that is required for note-taking for the legal memo. In addition to making connections between the law in the cases and the facts of the client's case for the purpose of resolv-

---

EXERCISE 11: Critically read & brief all of the legal authority that is necessary to resolve your client's case in the manner described in Section 1-2 for this chapter. Do not forget to label your cases appropriately. As you are reading, jot down any ideas you have about possible theories of the case that explain your client's conduct.

---

ing the client's legal issue(s), a legal reader must take the extra step of identifying which theories of the case support which connections. For example, a person comes to your office alleging that they were injured when they tripped over an object in the grocery store aisle. This is a cause of action involving negligence. You locate the proper legal authorities that concern this matter and critically read them. As you write your case briefs, you find that courts are more likely to rule for the plaintiff in similar situations when the customer was aware of their surroundings, the store personnel did not perform regular checks of the aisles for spills or debris, and/or the employees missed spills or debris even when conducting regular aisle inspections. When taking notes for your client's case, you would first identify the reasoning the courts used and the range of facts included in that reasoning when the court ruled both for and against the plaintiff. Next, you would determine which reasoning best encompassed your client's situation and develop a theory from it that explained your client's conduct.

EXERCISE 12: Using any of the note-taking methods explained previously (listing, free writing, or cubing) take notes on your client's case for the purpose of creating a legal brief. Be sure to (1) identify the reasoning the court used and the range of facts included in that reasoning when the court ruled for and against the party in your client's position (plaintiff or defendant); (2) determine which reasoning best encompasses your client's situation; and (3) write down a plausible theory or theories from that reasoning that explains your client's conduct.

MATERIALS: Examples of listing, free-writing, and cubing for creating a legal brief are in the Model Answers folder for this chapter under Exercise 12.

Organization and Synthesis

Organization

Prior to drafting the rules persuasively, you must develop a theory for your case. A theory of the case is the foundation for all of the authority and arguments formulated from that authority in your legal brief. In formulating your authority persuasively, you must place it within the context of your theory of the case. For example, in a case where your client tripped over an object in the grocery store aisle, your theory may be that the grocery store personnel were not conscientious in searching for or removing objects from the aisles that could cause injury to the store's customers. Your persuasive synthesis of authorities would need to support this theory. Do not move on until you have selected a plausible theory for your case.

As mentioned previously, the organization for any piece of writing depends on the overall purpose for the piece of writing. The rhetorical purpose of a persuasive synthesis of legal authorities is to advance the theory of the client's case through a careful explanation of the relevant legal authorities. Just like for the legal memo, you will need to sort the cases by cause of action, then by category or the particular issues they explore, and then by the concepts that the court elaborates on within each category. However, you will also need to identify which cases support your client's position and which do not, and develop a plan to discuss both in a manner that honestly conveys the court's reasoning but supports your theory of the case.

Again, you can accomplish these tasks by organizing the information in an outline or a MindMap. Regardless of which organizational tool you use, you will have to develop point headings or a series of arguments usually ordered inductively. Each point heading usually consists of an assertion about what you want the court to do or why your client should prevail, and then the brief reason for the assertion. Review the following point headings for our grocery store case ordered inductively:

> **Theory of the case:** *The grocery store personnel were not conscientious in searching for or removing objects from the aisles that could cause injury to the store's customers.*
>
> **Main Point Heading 1:** Mr. Y should prevail against Grocery Store, Inc. because he meets all of the elements required to prove that it was negligent.
>
> **Sub-Point Heading A:** Grocery Store, Inc. had a duty to Mr. Y, which it breached by failing to remove debris from Aisle 12.
>
> **Sub-Point Heading B:** Grocery Store, Inc.'s breach of its duty to Mr. Y was the cause of Mr. Y's injury.

EXERCISE 13: Develop point headings for your legal brief that support your theory of the case and advance your arguments on your client's behalf. After you have done so, arrange your relevant legal authorities and facts according to point heading using either an outline or MindMap. Pay attention to the legal authority that proves problematic for your case. Develop strategies for synthesizing those authorities in a manner that honestly portrays the court's reasoning and supports your theory of the case.

MATERIALS: Examples of an outline and MindMap for a legal brief are in the Model Answers folder for this chapter under Exercise 13.

Synthesis

When a lawyer synthesizes legal authority persuasively, he or she tests the boundaries that the court has set for a particular cause of action. In framing the cause of action through point headings and/or issue statements, the lawyer recategorizes the relevant legal category or categories to support the theory of the case as follows:

A. If a lawyer wants the precedent authority for a category to support the client's position and the facts of the case raise issues consistent with the precedent authority and the reasoning used to create that authority, then the lawyer will frame the issue(s) as it has been framed in the precedent authority. This strategy keeps the court's category for a cause of action intact. Simply, the lawyer's argument is "X issue is just like [the precedent authorities] because Y ..." The lawyer will then shape the legal synthesis to look like the precedent authorities in a manner that advances the theory of the case.

B. If a lawyer wants the precedent authority for a category to support the client's position, but the facts of the case raise issues inconsistent with the precedent authority and the reasoning used to create that authority, then the lawyer will frame the issue in a manner that includes it within the precedent authority. This strategy attempts to expand the court's category for a cause of action in accordance with the theory of the case. It is the "X issue is included in [the precedent authorities] because Y ..." argument. The lawyer will then shape the legal synthesis to include the new issue(s) in the precedent authorities.

C. If a lawyer <u>does not</u> want the precedent authority for a category to support the client's position, but the facts of the case raise issues consistent with the precedent authority and the reasoning used to create that authority, then the lawyer will frame the issue in a manner that sets it apart from the precedent authority. This strategy attempts to constrict the court's category for a cause of action in accordance with the theory of the case. In this instance, the lawyer will argue that "X issue is unlike or distinguishable from [the precedent authorities] because Y ..." The lawyer will then shape the legal synthesis to highlight the differences between the precedent authorities and their case.

D. If a lawyer <u>does not</u> want the precedent authority for a category to support the client's position, and the facts of the case raise issues inconsistent with the precedent authority and the reasoning used to create that authority, then the lawyer will frame the issue in a manner that reiterates to the court the boundaries of a category for a particular cause of action in accordance with the theory of the case. Such arguments take the shape of "X issue is excluded from [the precedent authorities] because Y ..." The lawyer will then shape the legal synthesis to reinforce the court's boundaries for a category and strongly demarcate where the court's boundaries end and the client's case begins.

Lawyers may use a combination of the strategies in A–D in developing their persuasive rule synthesis. Regardless of the strategy, the reader should be able to determine your theory of the case from a reading of your persuasive rule synthesis.

As you are determining how to present your rules persuasively, answer the following questions for each case:

1. *In framing the issue before it, has the court adopted the appellant's or appellee's argument, or has the court framed the issue in its own manner? Ultimately, how did the court frame the issue? (You must determine how the issue was framed for each legal category and the concepts within it.)*

2. *Do the facts of your case raise issues consistent with the precedent authority and the reasoning used to create it for the relevant legal categories and concepts? If so, what are they?*

   a. *How can you frame the issue in a manner that keeps the court's categories and concepts intact?*

   b. *How can you frame the issue in a manner that constricts the court's categories and concepts?*

3. *Do the facts of your case raise issues inconsistent with the precedent authority and the reasoning used to create it? If so, what are they?*

   a. *How can you frame the issue in a manner that expands the court's categories and concepts to include your case?*

   b. *How can you frame the issue in a manner that maintains the court's categories and concepts so as to exclude your case?*

In drafting your persuasive synthesis of the relevant legal authorities, you must do the following:

Determine the cause of action. *What area or areas of law does the cause of action involve?*

Categorize the authorities according to how you have re-categorized the relevant legal category or categories to support the theory of the case.

Define the category and its concepts in a manner that supports the theory of the case.

Compare and **Contrast** similarities and differences between the authorities using the major concepts from the authorities, organized by category.

Explain those similarities and differences in turn and how they impact your understanding of the relationship between authorities for the major concepts in each category. Your explanations must support the theory of the case.

<u>Understand</u> how those similarities and differences alter your reading of subsequent authorities.

<u>Connect</u> all of your explanations moving from concept to concept, category to category until you have exhausted all of your available relevant authority (primarily case law). YOU CANNOT IGNORE case law that is contrary to your position. Rather, you must explain adverse authority honestly and in a manner that supports the theory of the case. In explaining the concepts in the authorities, you may want to use factual illustrations from the cases if they aid in those explanations. If you do include factual illustrations, make sure that you organize them after a cohesive discussion of the relevant legal authorities. You want to make sure that the reader has a grasp on the resulting authority from the court's reasoning process before you use facts to illustrate conceptual threads within those authorities.

EXERCISE 14: Draft a persuasive synthesis of authorities or re-draft the objective synthesis of authorities from the *Model Memo* into a persuasive synthesis of authorities. Make sure that you use the strategies discussed above. Do not forget to give proper attribution to your legal authorities.

Analysis and Conclusions

Analysis

When a lawyer analyzes facts persuasively (builds arguments), they challenge whether those facts and the reasoning used to resolve issues involving those facts should be included or excluded from within the boundaries set by the persuasive synthesis for a particular cause of action. Following the categorization or re-categorization in the synthesis, the lawyer forms arguments to support the desired outcome as follows:

A. If a lawyer wants the precedent authority for a category to support their client's position, and the facts of the case raise issues consistent with the precedent authority and the reasoning used to create that authority, then the lawyer will make the facts of the case appear the same as or similar to the facts in the precedent authority by emphasizing the similarities and de-emphasizing the differences. Facts in the precedent authority that are similar to the facts of the case are called analogous case facts. The lawyer will also use the reasoning in the precedent authority to build arguments to resolve the issues raised by the facts of the case. The lawyer's argument is "Because the facts in the case are analogous to the facts in the legal authorities, this court should decide X issue by using the same reasoning it did in the precedent authorities."

B.   If a lawyer wants the precedent authority for a category to support their client's position, but the facts of the case raise issues inconsistent with the precedent authority and the reasoning used to create the precedent authority, then the lawyer must present the facts in a way that includes them within the scope of facts in the precedent authority. This strategy attempts to expand the universe of facts that the court will consider in resolving a particular cause of action so that the reasoning in the precedent authority can be utilized to resolve the issues raised by those facts. Essentially, the lawyer argues that "the facts of the case are really the same or similar to the facts in those cases where the reasoning in the precedent authority controlled the resolution of the issue." For this type of argument, the lawyer finds facts in the case to analogize to the facts in the precedent authorities.

C.   If a lawyer <u>does not</u> want the precedent authority for a category to support the client's position, but the facts of the case raise issues consistent with the precedent authority and the reasoning used to create that authority, then the lawyer will emphasize the points where the facts of the case seemingly diverge from the facts in the precedent authority and downplay the points where the facts seem to converge. The core of the lawyer's argument will be that "The facts in the case may seem similar to the facts in the precedent authority but are actually different because ..." The lawyer will then shape the legal analysis to highlight the differences between the precedent authority, the reasoning used to create that authority, and the facts of their case to make the reasoning in the precedent authority inapplicable to the case.

D.   If a lawyer <u>does not</u> want the precedent authority for a category to support their client's position, and the facts of the case raise issues inconsistent with the precedent authority and the reasoning used to create the precedent authority, then the lawyer will discuss the facts in the case in a manner that emphasizes how different those facts are from the facts in the precedent authority and the reasoning to resolve issues involving those facts. Such arguments take the shape of "The reasoning in the precedent authority cannot be used to resolve my client's legal issue because the facts of my client's case fall outside of the factual universe and scope of the reasoning usually employed to resolve issues raised in that factual universe." The lawyer will then construct the legal analysis to reinforce the court's boundaries for a category and concepts with respect to the facts regularly included and the reasoning used to resolve issues involving those facts. This strategy works strongly to demarcate where the court's boundaries end and the client's case begins.

Lawyers may use a combination of the strategies in A–D in developing their persuasive factual analysis/arguments.

As you are determining how to analyze the facts of your case persuasively, answer the following questions for the authorities you used to create your persuasive rule synthesis:

1. *In discussing the issue before it, how has the court discussed the relevant facts using the reasoning from the precedent authority to resolve the issues raised by those facts? You must determine how the relevant facts and reasoning were used for each legal category and concept.*

2. *Do the facts of your case raise issues consistent with the precedent authority for the relevant legal categories and concepts? If so what are they?*

   a. *How can you discuss the relevant facts from your case using the reasoning from the precedent authority in a manner that keeps the court's category in tact?*

   b. *How can you discuss the relevant facts from your case using the reasoning from the precedent authority in a manner that constricts the court's category?*

3. *Do the facts of your case raise issues inconsistent with the precedent authority? If so, what are they?*

   a. *How can you discuss the relevant facts from your case using the reasoning from the precedent authority in a manner that expands the court's category to include your case?*

   b. *How can you discuss the relevant facts from your case using the reasoning from the precedent authority in a manner that maintains the court's category so as to exclude your case?*

In drafting your persuasive analysis of the facts in the case, you must do the following:

1. <u>Categorize</u> the facts under the same categories you used in your persuasive synthesis of authorities based on the issue for which they are relevant. You will accomplish this in your analysis by simply following the organizational structure that you created in your persuasive synthesis of authorities. Where your synthesis for a particular concept within a particular

category ends, you should begin your persuasive analysis. As you begin your analysis, you will need to make a decision about whether you will use inductive reasoning (an assertion concluding how the court should decide this issue followed by reasons) or deductive reasoning (reasons leading to an assertion concluding how the court should decide this issue) for your analysis. This choice will influence how you draft your topic sentences for each category and concept that you analyze.

2. **Compare** and **Contrast** the facts in the case with the facts in the legal authorities starting with facts that are relevant for the first category and concept and then taking each subsequent category and concept in turn. Do not start your analysis of one concept and category before finishing your analysis of another. Be sure to complete numbers 2–5 for each category and concept.

3. **Explain** the relationships between those comparisons using the language from the persuasive synthesis of authorities. How do the facts meet the criteria set out in the persuasive synthesis of authorities? How do the facts not meet the criteria set out in the synthesis of authorities? Be sure to use the applicable strategy or strategies in A–D.

4. **Connect** all of the explanations moving from point to point, assertion to assertion, until all of the plausible explanations are exhausted FOR YOUR SIDE. Do not make opposing counsel's arguments for them but anticipate the arguments that they will make and neutralize them with your own.

5. **Conclude** based on the weight of your analysis. This is a one-sentence conclusion at the end of each concept, not the summary conclusion that will appear at the end of your brief.

EXERCISE 15: Using the persuasive synthesis that you drafted for Exercise 14, formulate arguments that employ the relevant strategies above and reinforce your theory of the case. Do not forget to give attribution to your legal and factual authorities.

Drafting the Statement of Facts

The *Statement of Facts* for your legal brief is not objective but persuasive. Instead of telling your audience about your client's case, you will tell your audience your client's story through your client's eyes. This does not mean that you are free to make legal conclusions (conclusions about the legal consequences of certain facts) or use hyperbole as you tell your client's story. On the contrary, you must draft a persuasive story for your client by emphasizing the facts that are in line with your version of the events and de-emphasizing those that are not. Do not forget to provide attribution for the facts throughout this section where necessary. All of the facts that you use in your arguments must appear in your *Statement of Facts*.

EXERCISE 16: Using either the facts in the case file assigned to you or the objective *Statement of Facts* in the *Model Memo*, draft or re-draft a persuasive statement of facts for your legal brief.

Conclusions

The purpose of the *Conclusion* section of the legal brief is to formally ask the court to grant your client the outcome they are seeking. It is typically a sentence, but can be longer (a paragraph) if the attorney has the space to remind the court of the most persuasive elements in the brief. After formally requesting the most plausible and desired outcome, the lawyer signs the brief and places the license number that he or she was given when admitted to practice law in the signature block.

PUTTING IT ALL TOGETHER:
Using the skills that you have learned for constructing a legal brief, complete the legal brief assignment for the case file assigned to you.

Section 1-6: Approaches to the Law School Exam

The law school exam requires all of the critical reading, note-taking, synthesis, and analysis skills that we have discussed thus far. Its rhetorical purpose is to test a law student's mastery of synthesizing the legal authorities for a particular legal subject through the factual analysis of a hypothetical legal dilemma. The majority of law school examinations are essay examinations or a combination of essay and multiple-choice exams. Our focus is the law school essay exam, as approaches to it employ the processes discussed in this book.

The typical first year law school curriculum at most law schools in the United States consists of the following courses: Legal Analysis and Writing, Contracts, Property, Civil Procedure, Torts, Criminal Law, and Constitutional Law. While a smattering of law schools require law professors to have a mid-term or other intermediate assessment of student skills during the semester or quarter, the majority of law schools only require professors to hold a single final examination at the end of the semester or quarter in which the course is taken. Essentially, this means that as a law student your entire grade or a majority percentage of your grade in a class taken in your first year of law school is determined by your performance on the final exam.

Preparing for the Law School Exam

Each week of a semester or quarter of law school is a week of preparation for the law school examination. A law student who hopes to be successful on an examination cannot wait until reading period or the day before the exam to prepare. Rather, preparation begins when a student receives their syllabus, text, and other materials for each class.

The Course Syllabus and Text

A syllabus for a course is a written version of the professor's plan for conveying the most essential information for the course to the students in the time allotted. Because all of the courses in the typical first year law curriculum are tested on the bar exam, the licensing exam for all attorneys given in each state, a professor usually designs the syllabus to cover the information for each subject that is likely to be tested on the bar exam. For this reason, a law professor has little flexibility to deviate from the syllabus and will usually cover the syllabus in its entirety over a semester or quarter.

Of equal importance to the syllabus in a law school course is the text that a professor selects for the course. A text that contains primarily cases, commentaries about the cases (called "notes"), and exercises utilizing those cases is called a casebook. Casebooks are commonly employed in classes that focus primarily on teaching an area of the law (*i.e.,* Contracts, Property, etc.) rather than the analytical processes required to utilize the law in a meaningful manner (*i.e.,* Legal Analysis and Writing).

When you receive a syllabus for a law school course, it is a good practice to read it through at least once to determine what topics in the course subject matter your professor plans to cover. After you have read through the syllabus to get a big picture of the course, then you should read the syllabus in tandem with the table of contents for your casebook. In many instances, the syllabus will track the organizational structure of the casebook.

As we discussed earlier in this chapter, a text is an object that an author deliberately builds. It is constructed of parts ordered in a certain manner for a specified purpose. You have to disassemble those parts and reassemble them for your purposes, but to do this, you must understand how the text is constructed.[12] When you are reviewing the table of contents for the text in tandem with your professor's syllabus, ask yourself the following questions:

1. In what order is the information conveyed in the text?

2. Is this order the same or different from how my professor orders the information in the syllabus? *If the order is different, ask your professor why they have chosen to reorder information in a particular manner.*

3. Does the syllabus cover all of the information listed in the text? *If not, ask the professor why they have chosen to omit or add additional information that the text does not cover.*

These questions will give you an overall feel for the structure of the course and how the professor will convey the information in the course to you on a weekly basis.

MATERIALS: A sample table of contents from a casebook is located in the Final Exam Preparation folder located in the Exercises & Materials for this chapter.

EXERCISE 17: Review the sample table of contents in the Final Exam Preparation folder. As you read through it, ask yourself questions 1 and 2 above.

---

12. HJORTSHOJ, *supra* note 7, at 130.

Reading and Note-taking for the Law School Exam

Reading

In reviewing the sample table of contents for the casebook, you may have noticed that the subject of the course was split into categories, and that under each of those categories was a sub-category and a listing of cases. Each of the cases listed within the sub-category is designed to advance the reader's understanding of the legal concepts for that category.

For example, the sample table of contents provided is from a casebook on contract law. The topic of Section 2, a sub-category of Chapter Two, is "Manifestation of Assent and the Objective Theory of Contracts." All of the cases listed under that sub-category are designed to advance the reader's understanding of "Manifestation of Assent and the Objective Theory of Contracts."

Note-taking

In addition to briefing the cases in preparation for the class session where they will be discussed, it is also necessary to take notes on the cases as they are discussed during class to connect their relationship to each other and their relationship as a whole to the other parts of the text and course syllabus. Such a practice will enable you to determine how each grouping of cases advances your understanding of the sub-category and category where it is located. Case briefing must be done in advance of class as preparation for the class session and then reviewed and supplemented with class notes sometime after the class session to integrate any new insights gained from the class session.

MATERIALS: A case brief template for class preparation is in the Final Exam Preparation folder located in the Exercises & Materials for this chapter.

EXERCISE 18: Using the techniques for case briefing described in Section 1-2 of this chapter and the case brief template for class preparation, brief the cases listed in the excerpted table of contents as provided for you in the Final Exam Preparation folder.

Synthesizing, Analyzing, and Organizing Information for the Law School Exam

Synthesis

As mentioned previously, each week of a syllabus builds on the last. Each week is designed to add to your understanding of the overall subject matter of the course though an exploration of the various categories and concepts within that subject matter. For example, the excerpted table of contents covers Chapter Two: Formation, Section 2: Manifestation of Assent and the Objective Theory of Contracts, and the following cases: *Lucy v. Zehmer, Leonard v. Pepsico, Inc., Stepp v. Freeman*, and *Anderson Investments, L.L.C. v. Factory Card Outlet of America, Ltd.* In order to understand the concepts that these cases are meant to convey, a law student must go beyond the case briefing and note-taking processes to synthesize each listing of cases in the categories and sub-categories in the text as assigned by the syllabus. Synthesizing case groupings throughout the semester or quarter for a course will allow you to build a cohesive understanding of the law as conveyed in a category and sub-category, and ultimately for the course subject matter as a whole. Not only will this practice allow you to review what you have learned each week, but it will also give you a deeper understanding of the substantive law in the course and aid you in preparing for the final exam in the course.

EXERCISE 19: Using the techniques for synthesizing legal authorities in Section 1-3 of this chapter, synthesize the cases listed in the excerpted table of contents provided in the Final Exam Preparation folder.

Analysis

Because of the frequency with which law school exams are given, there are not many chances throughout the semester or quarter for a law student to engage in factual analysis in a test-taking environment at regular intervals. However, the majority of casebooks have numerous notes, questions, and exercises on the pages after a case or series of cases in the book. The notes, questions, and exercises provide the law student with the opportunity to self-test on the concepts that the cases were meant to convey using the synthesis of the cases they create for a category or sub-category. For example, after revising the case briefs on the cases with course lecture notes and then synthesizing the cases for the week, a law student would then test their knowledge of the law in that category or sub-category by answering the questions or completing the exercises that appear at the end of it. This learning strategy allows a student to pinpoint places where their understanding of the law is shaky and affords them the time to re-read the cases for a greater understanding of the law and/or ask their professor questions to clear up any ambiguities.

EXERCISE 20: Using the techniques for factual analysis in Section 1-4 of this chapter, complete a factual analysis of the note "Who's Joking?" in the Final Exam Preparation folder.

Organization as Preparation for the Law School Exam

The organization of all of your mini-syntheses for each category and sub-category of a course's subject matter, as well as any supplemental information, is one of the final steps in the exam preparation process. Your goal in organizing the information is to provide yourself with a roadmap through the course that leads to you to a comprehensive understanding of the body of law in the course. For example, your organization of information for a Contracts course should give you a comprehensive understanding of the law in each of the categories and sub-categories, the body of law for the course, you covered over the semester or quarter. Although most law students choose an outline format to organize the information in a course, you must choose the format that is best for you.

MATERIALS: A sample outline and MindMap for exam preparation are in the Final Exam Preparation folder located in the Exercises & Materials for this chapter.

Most law school exams are closed-book examinations and you will usually not be permitted to bring your outline or any other course materials to the exam with you. However, the process of weekly note-taking and synthesizing, in addition to the final process of organizing all of the information in the course by category and sub-category will help to ensure that you have properly synthesized the law and are able to use it as your framework for any factual analysis required on an exam.

EXERCISE 21: Organize the mini-syntheses (as supplemented by your notes) into an outline or MindMap. Use the excerpted table of contents and the syllabus as your guide.

The final step in the exam preparation process is to practice writing exam essays, first in an un-timed and then in a timed environment. You may ask your professor for practice exams and review your casebook to determine if it has any practice exams.

Writing the Law School Exam Answer

The law school essay exam is a hypothetical factual situation(s) involving the subject matter of the course that concludes with a question that the examiner wants you to answer. The question may ask you to resolve all of the legal issues suggested by the facts, discuss any causes of action that a party may bring, discuss any causes of action that may be brought against a party, or to discuss the arguments for and against the parties involved. Regardless of what the question(s) asks, your answer must demonstrate to your professor that you are able to spot the legal issues suggested by a group of facts, communicate the appropriate set of legal rules necessary to resolve the issues accurately and in a synthesized form, use the synthesis as a framework to analyze the legally relevant facts, and adequately address the resolution to the legal issues succinctly in your essay conclusion.

Reading and Note-taking for the Law School Exam Answer

Probably the most important step required to write an essay exam answer is actually reading the exam. The first read through of an essay exam is to get a basic sense of the facts and the legal question(s) that the examiner asks. On each subsequent read through, the reader reads critically by engaging the text of the exam with the following three questions: What are the legal issues suggested by the facts? What law is necessary to resolve the legal issue(s)? and What are the legally relevant facts?

The notes that the reader takes on these questions can be in any form. Their overall purpose is to give the reader the opportunity to make sense of the exam question and to provide information that the reader can organize in preparing to write the exam.

MATERIALS: A sample exam question and a version of it annotated as a critical reading dialogue are in the Final Exam Preparation folder located in the Exercises & Materials for this chapter.

The written structure for a law essay exam is similar to the structure for a legal memo.

Corresponding Parts of an Exam Answer and Legal Memo

Parts of an Exam Answer	Parts of a Legal Memo
Spot the legal issues suggested by a group of facts	Question(s) Presented
Communicate the appropriate set of legal rules necessary to resolve the issues accurately and in a synthesized form	Discussion Section: Synthesis of Legal Authorities
Use the synthesis as a framework to analyze the legally relevant facts	Discussion Section: Factual Analysis
Adequately address the resolution to the legal issues succinctly in the essay conclusion	Short Answer(s); Conclusion

Because most law school exams are administered in a three to four hour time period, a response to an essay question cannot be as detailed as the legal memo. The issue is often stated simply as the legal question you are asked to resolve. The synthesis resembles the mini-syntheses in your outline and not the detailed case synthesis for a memo. This is true not only because of time constraints but also because of the nature of the closed-book exam. Closed-book examinations restrict you to the information in your head. The analysis most closely resembles its memo counterpart. It must be thorough and exhaust all of the possible law and legally significant facts. Generally, the exam conclusion is more succinct than the *Conclusion* that appears in the memo. However, depending on what the essay question asks, the conclusion might resemble the full *Conclusion* at the end of the memo or the *Short Answer*.

Unless a professor instructs otherwise, the typical law school exam answer is structured as follows:

Issue: What is the legal question(s) that I am being asked to resolve?

Rule: Which of the mini-syntheses that I created is applicable to resolving the legal issue?

Analysis: How can I resolve the legal issue by using my mini-synthesis as a framework for my factual analysis of the relevant facts in the essay question?

Conclusion: What is the answer(s) to the legal questions(s) that I am being asked to resolve?

As this is the most common exam answer structure, it makes sense to organize the information in your notes in this structure for each of issues you must answer on the exam.

On average, the reading, note-taking, and organization strategies for a law school exam take ¼ to ⅓ of the total exam time allotted. However, utilizing these strategies will result in a thorough and well-organized answer. As you write your answer in an actual or simulated exam environment, be mindful of the time that you have remaining and be sure to leave yourself time to read through the exam for any grammatical errors.

PUTTING IT ALL TOGETHER:

Using the skills that you have learned for writing the law school essay exam answer, write an answer to the exam question provided for you in the Final Exam Preparation folder.

Section 1-7: Exercises & Materials List

This section corresponds to the Exercises & Materials folder located on the CD-ROM that accompanies this text. The following folders and their contents are located within the Exercises & Materials folder for this chapter:

Reading and Note-taking

1. Example of a Statute: *"Dyeing or selling dyed baby fowl or rabbits"*

2. Example of a Statutory Diagram: *"Dyeing or selling dyed baby fowl or rabbits"*

3. Statute for Exercise 2: *"Unlawful bear exploitation"*

4. Labeled Case Example (critical reading dialogue): *Stambovsky v. Ackley (crd)*

5. Standard Case Brief Template
6. Sample Case Brief: *Stambovsky v. Ackley*
7. Labeled Case (with parts of a case brief): *Stambovsky v. Ackley (cb)*
8. Labeled Case (with parts of a legal memo): *Stambovsky v. Ackley (lm)*

Organization and Synthesis

Please Note: All examples of Organization and Synthesis for materials in the Nickety case are located in the Model Answers folder for this chapter.

Legal Memo Case File (Persia Nickety v. J-Mart, Inc.*)*

1. Assigning Memo
2. Telephone Interview with Persia Nickety
3. Legal Authority for the Nickety Case
4. Standard Legal Memo Template
5. Directions for Drafting Questions Presented and Short Answers

Legal Brief Case File

1. Assigning Memo
2. Additional Legal Authority for the Nickety Case
3. Standard Legal Brief Template

Final Exam Preparation

1. Sample Table of Contents from a Casebook
2. Standard Case Brief Template for Outlining and Class Preparation
3. Cases for Final Exam Preparation
4. Sample Final Exam Outline
5. Sample Final Exam MindMap
6. Sample Note—Who's Joking?
7. Sample Final Exam Question
8. Sample Final Exam Question (Annotated)

Chapter Two

Legal Writing from a Social Scientist's Perspective

"The only possible interpretation of any research whatever in the 'social sciences' is: some do, some don't."[13]

—Ernest Rutherford

Section 2-1: The Legal Memo— Legal Writing to Inform

Social scientists explore various aspects of human society such as social inequality, political behavior, wealth distribution, social class development, management and creation of space, mental behavior, and human social action and interaction. The Social Sciences are made up of the following disciplines: political science, sociology, history (also included as a discipline in the Humanities), psychology (also included in the Sciences), anthropology, economics, communications, and linguistics. Social scientists utilize variants of the scientific method to study society. They first identify a problem, form hypotheses or questions about the problem, test those hypotheses, and analyze the results of the test.[14] Their methodology can be divided into two categories: the search for data and the analysis of data. Social scientists use empirical research, historical research, interviews, participant observation, surveys, and case studies to collect data relevant to the identified problem and hypothesis. They then analyze this data through quantitative analysis (the representation of results

---

13. ThinkExist.com Quotations, http://thinkexist.com/quotation/the_only_possible_conclusion_the_social_sciences/196621.html.

14. Lee Cuba, A Short Guide to Writing About Social Sciences 82–83 (4th ed. 2002); Gregory M. Scott & Stephen M. Garrison, The Political Science Student Writer's Manual 79 (4th ed. 2002).

numerically), theories, statistical analysis, and qualitative analysis (the subjective assessment of non-quantifiable data).[15]

Social scientists communicate their data collection and analysis through the following types of writing: research papers (based on empirical research, library research, and/or archival research), case studies, and analysis papers. They may also create and/or utilize book reviews, article critiques, literature reviews, reaction/response papers, and position papers to aid them in constructing research papers, case studies, and analysis papers.

The Social Science Research Paper and Case Study

A typical research paper and case study in the social sciences has the following parts:

1. Title Page
2. Abstract (if appropriate)
3. Introduction/statement of the problem
4. Research Methodology
5. Findings/Results
6. Discussion/conclusions
7. Notes (if appropriate)
8. References
9. Appendixes (if appropriate)[16]

For research papers that do not involve empirical research, the author will keep the introduction section (number 3) but may integrate numbers 4–6 into one large section that forms the body of the paper. Also, the author may combine sections and omit others in drafting papers using empirical research or library research. Because the structure of these papers may change according to author, it is important to focus on the rhetorical purpose of the paper sections rather than the headings assigned to them.

---

15. CUBA, *supra* note 14, at 82–83; SCOTT & GARRISON, *supra* note 14, at 80.
16. CUBA, *supra* note 14, at 82–83; SCOTT & GARRISON, *supra* note 14, at 65.

Section 2-2: Reading and Note-taking Strategies for Legal Authorities

Reading

In order to actively engage with the types of texts that social scientists write, it is necessary to review the general structure of those common texts, their overall rhetorical purpose, and the rhetorical purpose of each of their parts. The overall rhetorical purpose of any social science research paper or case study is to answer a question.[17] In developing a research paper or case study, a writer answers the question through collecting data, empirically or through library research, and analyzing that data based on a framework developed from evaluating the empirical data, the research of others, or both. Each part of the research paper or case study has the following rhetorical purpose:[18]

1. **Title Page:** *States the topic of the paper.*

2. **Abstract (if appropriate):** *Concisely summarizes the major research findings and the author's analysis of them.*

3. **Introduction/statement of the problem:** *Explains the hypothesis or questions that focus the study, the theory or thesis for the research findings, and locates the research within a disciplinary context.*

4. **Research Methodology:** *Explains the process for collecting and analyzing data in enough detail so that subsequent researchers can replicate it.*

5. **Findings/Results:** *Synthesizes the research findings for each hypothesis or part of the thesis.*

6. **Discussion/conclusions:** *Uses inductive or deductive reasoning to make sense of the research findings in light of the hypothesis or thesis.*

7. **Notes (if appropriate):** *Give attribution to the sources used in endnote, footnote, or other form.*

8. **References:** *Generally cites all of the works used in the paper.*

9. **Appendixes (if appropriate):** *Contains materials that further illustrate any of the paper concepts or details.*

---

17. Cuba, *supra* note 14, at 82–83; Scott & Garrison, *supra* note 14, at 79.

18. Anne Merle Feldman, Writing and Learning in the Disciplines 90–92, 492–493 (1996); Cuba, *supra* note 14, at 85–119.

MATERIALS: Examples of a case study and research paper using empirical research, and a research paper using library research are in the Reading and Note-taking folder located in the Exercises & Materials for this chapter as Case Study #1: *The adequacy of policy responses to the treatment needs of South Africans living with HIV (1999–2008)*; Research Paper #1: *Congressional Trends to Tax and Spend: Examining Fiscal Voting Across Time and Chamber*, and Library Research Paper #1: *Hol(e)y Statues: Some reflections on holes, emptiness and longing in the work of two Australian émigré sculptors of the fifties.*

Corresponding Parts of a Social Science Research Paper and Case Study Using Empirical Research and a Legal Memo

Parts of a Social Science Research Paper Using Empirical Research and a Case Study	Parts of a Legal Memo
Title Page	"RE:" in memo caption; Short description of the client's case at the beginning of the memo
Abstract and/or Executive Summary	Short Answer; Conclusion *(if an Executive Summary)*
Introduction/statement of the problem	Question(s) Presented; Discussion Section: Synthesis of Legal Authorities
Research methodology	Discussion Section: Synthesis of Legal Authorities
Findings/results	Statement of Facts
Discussion/conclusions	Discussion Section: Synthesis of Legal Authorities; Discussion Section: Factual Analysis; Conclusion
Notes *(APA, ASA, Chicago Manual of Style)*	*Bluebook* or *ALWD* citation form
References	N/A
Appendixes	Same *(if applicable)*

MATERIALS: Examples of a case study and research paper using empirical research labeled with the corresponding parts of a legal memo are in the Reading and Note-taking folder located in the Exercises & Materials for this chapter as Case Study #1A: *The adequacy of policy responses to the treatment needs of South Africans living with HIV (1999–2008)*; and Research Paper #1A: *Congressional Trends to Tax and Spend: Examining Fiscal Voting Across Time and Chamber.*

Corresponding Parts of a Social Science Research Paper
Using Library Research and a Legal Memo

Parts of a Social Science Research Paper Using Library Research	Parts of a Legal Memo
Title or Title Page	"RE:" in memo caption; Short description of the client's case at the beginning of the memo
Introduction/statement of problem	Question(s) Presented; Discussion Section: Synthesis of Legal Authorities; Short Answer
Research methodology *(may or may not be included)*	Discussion Section: Synthesis of Legal Authorities
Body/Discussion	Statement of Facts; Discussion Section: Synthesis of Legal Authorities; Discussion Section: Factual Analysis
Conclusion	Short Answer; Conclusion
Notes *(APA, ASA, Chicago Manual of Style)*	*Bluebook* or *ALWD* citation form
References	N/A
Appendixes *(may or may not be included)*	Same *(if applicable)*

MATERIALS: An example of a research paper using library research labeled with the corresponding parts of a legal memo is in the Reading and Note-taking folder located in the Exercises & Materials for this chapter as Library Research Paper #1A: *Hol(e)y Statues: Some reflections on holes, emptiness and longing in the work of two Australian émigré sculptors of the fifties.*

EXERCISE 1: Label the social science article *We Do Not Enjoy Equal Political Rights: Ghanaian Women's Perceptions on Political Participation in Ghana* by identifying the parts that correspond to the parts of a legal memo and by explaining the rhetorical purpose of each part. The article is located under Exercise 1 in the Reading and Note-taking folder.

EXERCISE 2: Label one of the cases in the Legal Memo Case File with the parts that correspond to the parts of the social science article/research paper.

Note-taking

Developing a Research Question

To grasp the meaning of a text, social scientists actively read the text and take notes on it while they are reading it. Whether conducting empirical or library research, social scientists formulate a research question, a question that they hope to have answered through the research, in advance of conducting the research. Through the research, that question often evolves into a hypothesis or a thesis.

The research process itself often refines research questions. A social science researcher may begin the research with questions about a particular social problem, but then may further focus the question after conducting empirical research or library research. After completing empirical or library research, the author is ready to draft the introduction to the paper. An author drafting a paper introduction conducts the following rhetorical moves:

1. Establishes the field in which the study falls or explains the disciplinary context;

2. Summarizes the relevant research for the subject of the study;

3. Creates a space for their research by indicating gaps in the relevant research or by raising questions about that research; and

4. Introduces the study by noting the contribution it will make to the field.[19]

---

19. Carol Berkenkotter, Thomas N. Huckin & John Ackerman, *Social Context in Socially Constructed Texts: The Initiation of a Graduate Student into a Writing Research Community, in* TEXTUAL DYNAMICS OF THE PROFESSIONS: HISTORICAL AND CONTEMPORARY STUDIES OF WRITING IN PROFESSIONAL COMMUNITIES 196 (Charles Bazerman & James Paradis eds., 1991).

Corresponding Parts of an Introduction and Legal Memo

Parts of the Introduction	Parts of a Legal Memo
Establishes the field in which the study falls or explains the disciplinary context	Question Presented: States the area of law that the case involves
Summarizes the relevant research for the subject of the study	Question Presented: States the particular legal question that the memo seeks to answer
Creates a space for their research by indicating gaps in the relevant research or by raising questions about that research	Question Presented: States the facts of the client's case that are important to resolving that question
Introduces the study by noting the contribution it will make to the field	Short Answer

Engaging with the Texts

When taking notes on the texts they read, social scientists ask themselves the following questions:

1. What is the topic of the reading?
2. What is the subject of the reading? *(The subject of the empirical or library research.)*
3. What is the author's hypothesis or thesis? What insight does the hypothesis or thesis give us into the research questions that the author sought to answer by the research?
4. What support does the author give for the hypothesis or thesis?
5. Are the sources of support adequate? Why or why not?
6. What kind of conclusions does the author make based on the outcome of the research?
7. After completing the reading, what have I learned? Did the author adequately support the hypothesis or thesis?

These questions allow the author to determine the major category or categories in which the text falls, ascertain the major concepts within the category or categories that the author explores, and evaluate whether the author has adequately explored the concepts and supported any assertions made about the concepts. They also help the author to further refine their research question and, eventually, the introduction to the paper containing the hypothesis or thesis.

The research questions correspond to the types of questions that lawyers ask when reading and briefing a case.

Reading Questions and their Case Brief Counterparts

Reading Questions	Parts of a Case Brief
What is the topic of the reading?	Procedural Posture
What is the subject of the reading?	Facts
What is the author's hypothesis or thesis?	Issue(s)
What support does the author give for the hypothesis or thesis?	*Ratio Decidendi*: Synthesis of Legal Authorities (Rule)
Are the sources of support adequate? Why or why not?	*Ratio Decidendi*: Factual Analysis
What kind of conclusions does the author make based on the outcome of the research?	Ruling
After completing the reading, what have I learned? Did the author adequately support the hypothesis or thesis?	Holding

---

EXERCISE 3: For the social science article in Exercise 1, *We Do Not Enjoy Equal Political Rights: Ghanaian Women's Perceptions on Political Partici-pation in Ghana,* answer the reading questions. After you have finished, label the social science article by identifying the parts that correspond to the parts of a case brief. For the introduction portion of the paper, label the parts that correspond to the rhetorical moves an author makes in developing the Question(s) Presented and Short Answer(s) portions of the memo.

Complete **EXERCISES 4, 5**, and **6** in Chapter 1.

Section 2-3: Organizing and Synthesizing Legal Authorities

A synthesis of sources is more than a summary of sources, although it does include summaries of sources within it. Rather, it is the organization of research sources or authorities by category, and the explanation of the similarities and differences between the sources in each category, arranged by concept.[20] This structure is mimicked in the social sciences in the compare-contrast essay, organized point-by-point or by block, and in the general idea of the synthesis essay.[21] The main difference between the synthesis of legal authorities and the synthesis of compare-contrast essays in the social sciences is that in the latter, the author interweaves their opinions about the authorities throughout the text. In legal writing, an evaluation of the sources is not interwoven throughout the synthesis of legal authorities because the rhetorical purpose of the legal synthesis is to provide an objective framework to analyze the facts of the client's case. Its purpose is not to advocate for a particular point of view. For legal authors, the process of evaluation occurs in the analysis section of the legal memo, which we will discuss in Section 2-4 of this chapter.

To determine how the compare-contrast essay is similar to the synthesis of legal authorities, a closer examination of its structure is necessary. Under the point-by-point structure of the compare-contrast essay, the author separates the essay into categories and then, within each category, lists the major concepts. For each of the research authorities relevant to a particular concept, the writer explains the similarities and differences between them. In explaining the similarities and differences between the authorities, the author summarizes, paraphrases, and quotes them.

---

20. MARY LYNCH KENNEDY, WILLIAM J. KENNEDY & HADLEY M. SMITH, WRITING IN THE DISCIPLINES: A READER FOR WRITERS 83–86, 96–100, (4th ed. 1996).
21. *Id.*

Outline of a Compare-Contrast Essay Organized Point by Point

Topic: Predictors of Academic Success for Teens

Working Thesis: Teen, parental, and societal expectations concerning self-esteem, peer pressure, and educational opportunities are all predictors of teen academic success.

Authorities used: Smith, Jones, and Ward

Introduction

I.   Personal Expectations (CATEGORY 1)

    A.   Self-Esteem (Concept A)—What does each author say about this concept? What are the similarities and differences between each author's assertions?

    B.   Peer Pressure (Concept B)—What does each author say about this concept? What are the similarities and differences between each author's assertions?

    C.   Educational Opportunities (Concept C)—What does each author say about this concept? What are the similarities and differences between each author's assertions?

II. Parental Expectations (CATEGORY 2)

    A.   Self-Esteem (Concept A)—What does each author say about this concept? What are the similarities and differences between each author's assertions?

    B.   Peer Pressure (Concept B)—What does each author say about this concept? What are the similarities and differences between each author's assertions?

    C.   Educational Opportunities (Concept C)—What does each author say about this concept? What are the similarities and differences between each author's assertions?

III. Societal Expectations (CATEGORY 3)

    A.   Self-Esteem (Concept A)—What does each author say about this concept? What are the similarities and differences between each author's assertions?

    B.   Peer Pressure (Concept B)—What does each author say about this concept? What are the similarities and differences between each author's assertions?

    C.   Educational Opportunities (Concept C)—What does each author say about this concept? What are the similarities and differences between each author's assertions?

For the block structure, the author first separates the essay by the number of relevant authorities. Under each authority, the author further separates the essay into the categories that each authority discusses and then by concepts within those categories. In the block structure, the author discusses the authorities in turn, explaining the similarities and differences in the categories and concepts as the essay progresses. The author's explanation of the similarities and differences between the authorities requires summaries, paraphrases, and quotations from them.

Outline of a Compare-Contrast Essay Organized by Block

Topic: Predictors of Academic Success for Teens

Working Thesis: Teen, parental, and societal expectations concerning self-esteem, peer pressure, and educational opportunities are all predictors of teen academic success.

Authorities used: Smith, Jones, and Ward

Introduction

I. Smith

    A. Personal Expectations (CATEGORY 1)

        1. Self-Esteem (Concept A)

        2. Peer Pressure (Concept B)

        3. Educational Opportunities (Concept C)

    B. Parental Expectations (CATEGORY 2)

        1. Self-Esteem (Concept A)

        2. Peer Pressure (Concept B)

        3. Educational Opportunities (Concept C)

    C. Societal Expectations (CATEGORY 3)

        1. Self-Esteem (Concept A)

        2. Peer Pressure (Concept B)

        3. Educational Opportunities (Concept C)

II. Jones

    A. Personal Expectations (CATEGORY 1)

        1. Self-Esteem (Concept A)

        2. Peer Pressure (Concept B)

        3. Educational Opportunities (Concept C)

    B. Parental Expectations (CATEGORY 2)

        1. Self-Esteem (Concept A)

        2. Peer Pressure (Concept B)

        3. Educational Opportunities (Concept C)

    C. Societal Expectations (CATEGORY 3)

        1. Self-Esteem (Concept A)

        2. Peer Pressure (Concept B)

        3. Educational Opportunities (Concept C)

III. Ward (Omitted)

MATERIALS: Examples of the point-by-point and block outlines above in MindMap form are in the Organization and Synthesis folder located in the Exercises & Materials for this chapter.

A good example of a synthesis of authorities in social science writing is the literature review. As mentioned above, literature reviews are building blocks for research papers and are sometimes included in them. The literature review allows an author to get a sense of major conversations, or the discourse, in which the authors in their discipline are engaging. After reading the sources engaging in various conversations, authors can then decide if they wish to enter the conversation, critique the conversation, or start a new conversation where none exists. In this sense, literature reviews, like syntheses of legal authorities for legal memos, are foundational for research papers and case studies; they provide the basis for an author to determine and apply an existing framework to empirical or library research, or the basis for an author to create a framework to apply to empirical or library research.

EXERCISE 4: Using your case briefs and notes from Chapter 1, Section 1-3, construct an outline or MindMap for your synthesis of legal authorities that organizes your authorities in both a point-by-point and block format. Which format is better suited to conveying the meaning of the authorities to the reader? Why?

Complete **EXERCISES 7** and **8** in Chapter 1.

Section 2-4: Using Legal Authorities to Analyze Facts and to Develop Conclusions

Analysis

When social scientists analyze and evaluate texts, they break those texts into parts and methodically examine the parts to discern what they mean and how well they convey that meaning.[22] In examining the parts of the texts, so-

---

22. Feldman, *supra* note 18, at 481; Kennedy et al., *supra* note 20, at 132, 148.

cial scientists evaluate their strengths and weaknesses according to predetermined criteria designed to assess the structure and/or content of the text.[23] Usually, the criteria for evaluation follow the hypothesis/thesis/introduction of the social science research paper or case study. For example, after conducting empirical research or library research on young adult engagement in the election process, a social scientist may develop the thesis: *Social media is the most effective way to engage young people in the election process.* In constructing his or her analysis and evaluation, the social scientist will pick sources that support that thesis and/or carefully select examples from their library and/or empirical research to further support and illustrate their thesis. In this sense, the thesis or focus of the paper drives the analytical and evaluation processes.

In a longer research paper, an article, a social scientist may incorporate a literature review into the actual text of the article to aid in the evaluative and analytical processes. By using the review in this way, the author seeks to accomplish two tasks. The first is to situate their study into the discourse of the discipline, usually achieved by incorporating a major strain of the discourse or articulating a departure from the discourse in the thesis. The second is to use the review as a jumping off point, a reference, for the support the author will give to the thesis.

Let's review Case Study #1: *The adequacy of policy responses to the treatment needs of South Africans living with HIV (1999–2008)*; Research Paper #1:*Congressional Trends to Tax and Spend: Examining Fiscal Voting Across Time and Chamber;* and Library Research Paper #1: *Hol(e)y Statues: Some reflections on holes, emptiness and longing in the work of two Australian émigré sculptors of the fifties* for their analytical and evaluative characteristics.

Factual analysis in a legal memo involves both processes of analysis and evaluation. Factual analysis in the legal memo differs from the analysis and evaluation of social science texts in that the synthesis of legal authorities, including illustrations using facts from those authorities, is the sole criterion for evaluating the facts of a client's case. Remember, the rhetorical purpose of the legal synthesis is not persuasive like its social science counterpart but objective.

Complete **EXERCISES 9** and **10** in Chapter 1.

---

23. FELDMAN, *supra* note 18, at 481; KENNEDY ET AL., *supra* note 20, at 132, 148.

Developing Conclusions

For social scientists, the evaluation portion of the analytical process is where they make a judgment about whether the criteria for evaluation have been met. A summary of that judgment is placed in the conclusion of the paper, along with how the research findings contribute to the field of research as a whole. Similarly, the author of a legal memo follows the analytical process to a final conclusion that thoroughly discusses how the criteria for evaluation have or have not been met.

PUTTING IT ALL TOGETHER:
Using the skills that you have learned for building a legal memo, complete the legal memo assignment for the case file assigned to you.

Section 2-5: The Legal Brief— Legal Writing to Persuade

Before beginning to read this section, review the Legal Brief Case File in the Exercises & Materials for Chapter One.

Complete **EXERCISES 11** and **12** in Chapter 1.

Organization

As we discussed in the section on the legal memo, all social science writing seeks to answer a question. That question is informed by the social scientist's point of view about a topic. The point of view shapes the question into a thesis or hypothesis that advocates for or subscribes to a particular point of view. Most social science writing is not objective, giving equal time to opposing points of view. Rather the writer articulates an argument in the hypothesis or thesis and uses that hypothesis or thesis to focus the sources of authority and evidence to support it. In this sense, social science writing at its core is most similar to persuasive legal writing.

We examined the previous examples of social science writing to determine how the writer developed a literature review, a type of synthesis, as a building block for a research paper or case study, how the writer developed criteria to analyze and evaluate the subject of the study, and how the writer conducted that analysis and evaluation. In each of the social science excerpts, the writer linked the types of evidence to the arguments they made all for the purpose of supporting the thesis or hypothesis. Let's examine Case Study #1, Research Paper #1, and Library Research Paper #1 for their persuasive characteristics. Notice how all of the topic sentences for each major point support the hypothesis or thesis. These sentences mirror point headings in a legal brief. Notice how the support for the points refers to key portions of the literature review and/or examples from the subject of study. This portion of the paper mirrors the persuasive synthesis portion of the legal brief.

The argumentative structure of the excerpt examples and pieces of writing like it correlate to the parts of a legal brief:

Corresponding Parts of a Social Science Research Paper Using Empirical Research, Case Study, and Legal Brief

Parts of a Social Science Research Paper or Case Study Using Empirical Research	Parts of a Legal Brief
Title Page	Notice of Motion or Cover Sheet
Abstract and/or Executive Summary	Table of Contents; Conclusion
Introduction/statement of problem	Introduction
Research methodology	Motion Standard of Review; Argument: Persuasive Rule Synthesis
Findings/results	Statement of Facts
Discussion/conclusions	Argument: Persuasive Rule Synthesis; Argument: Factual Analysis/Argument; Conclusion
Notes (*APA, ASA, Chicago Manual of Style*)	*Bluebook* or *ALWD* citation form
References	Table of Authorities (*if included*)
Appendixes	Same (*if included*)

MATERIALS: Examples of a case study and research paper using empirical research labeled with the corresponding parts of a legal brief are in the Reading and Note-taking folder located in the Exercises & Materials for this chapter as Case Study #1B: *The adequacy of policy responses to the treatment needs of South Africans living with HIV (1999–2008)*; and Research Paper #1B: *Congressional Trends to Tax and Spend: Examining Fiscal Voting Across Time and Chamber.*

Corresponding Parts of a Social Science Research Paper Using Library Research and Legal Brief

Parts of a Social Science Research Paper Using Library Research	Parts of a Legal Brief
Title Page	Notice of Motion or Cover Sheet
Introduction/statement of problem	Introduction
Research methodology *(may or may not be included)*	Motion Standard of Review; Argument: Persuasive Rule Synthesis
Body/Discussion	Statement of Facts; Argument: Factual Analysis/Argument
Conclusion	Conclusion
Notes *(APA, ASA, Chicago Manual of Style)*	*Bluebook* or *ALWD* citation form
References	Table of Authorities *(if included)*
Appendixes *(may or may not be included)*	Same *(if applicable)*

MATERIALS: An example of a research paper using library research labeled with the corresponding parts of a legal brief is in the Reading and Note-taking folder located in the Exercises & Materials for this chapter as Library Research Paper #1B: *Hol(e)y Statues: Some reflections on holes, emptiness and longing in the work of two Australian émigré sculptors of the fifties.*

EXERCISE 5: Label the social science article for Exercise 1, *We Do Not Enjoy Equal Political Rights: Ghanaian Women's Perceptions on Political Participation in Ghana*, with the parts that correspond to the parts of a legal brief.

Complete **EXERCISE 13** in Chapter 1.

Synthesis

As mentioned previously, social scientists construct syntheses either for informational purposes or as support for arguments that they make in a research paper or case study. For example, in writing a literature review supporting a larger research work, social scientists carefully choose the sources they will use based on the discourse they are entering. Regardless of whether the author is aligning himself or herself with a particular conversation on a given subject or diverging from commonly held beliefs about a subject, the author must engage with the previous authors who have covered the same or similar subject. Such engagement requires the social scientist to anticipate the multiple ways in which research texts can be read, and during the writing process, to focus those sources to emphasize the portions that support the hypothesis or thesis and de-emphasize the portions that do not. The author may emphasize key portions of the text by placing summaries, paraphrases, or quotes of it in prominent places in the paper or by repeating key phrases from the research texts that directly support the hypothesis or thesis. During this process of focusing the authorities, writers must also decide how they will explain research that runs contrary to their hypothesis or thesis in a manner that does not undermine it. Note how the author constructs a persuasive synthesis of the sources in Library Research Paper #1.

Complete **EXERCISE 14** in Chapter 1.

Analysis and Conclusions

When social scientists analyze empirical or library research, they evaluate the strengths and weaknesses of that research using a hypothesis or thesis as criterion for evaluation. During the process of evaluation, the author makes assertions about why the research does or does not conform to the hypothesis or thesis, and supports those assertions with reasons and examples from the research. These reasons are ordered either inductively (reasons follow assertions concluding that the research conforms or does not conform to the thesis or hypothesis) or deductively (reasons lead to assertions concluding that the research conforms or does not conform to the thesis or hypothesis). Just as when the writer decided how to emphasize positive research authority and de-emphasize negative research authority in constructing the persuasive synthesis, the writer must also decide how to emphasize research results that support the thesis and de-emphasize those results that do not. Likewise, in building an analysis the author must decide how to refute counter-arguments that undermine the thesis or explain research findings that could be construed as disproving a hypothesis.

Complete **EXERCISES 15** and **16** in Chapter 1.

PUTTING IT ALL TOGETHER:
Using the skills that you have learned for constructing a legal brief, complete the legal brief assignment for the case file assigned to you.

Section 2-6: Exercises & Materials List

This section corresponds to the Exercises & Materials folder located on the CD-ROM that accompanies this text. The following folders and their contents are located within the Exercises & Materials folder for this chapter:

Reading and Note-taking

1. Case Study #1: *The adequacy of policy responses to the treatment needs of South Africans living with HIV (1999–2008)*

2. Research Paper #1: *Congressional Trends to Tax and Spend: Examining Fiscal Voting Across Time and Chamber*

3. Library Research Paper #1: *Hol(e)y Statues: Some reflections on holes, emptiness and longing in the work of two Australian émigré sculptors of the fifties.*

4. Case Study #1A: *Case Study #1 labeled with the parts of a legal memo*

5. Research Paper #1A: *Research Paper #1 labeled with the parts of a legal memo*

6. Library Research Paper #1A: *Library Research Paper #1 labeled with the parts of a legal memo*

7. Article for Exercise 1: *We Do Not Enjoy Equal Political Rights: Ghanaian Women's Perceptions on Political Participation in Ghana*

8. Case Study #1B: *Case Study #1 labeled with the parts of a legal brief*

9. Research Paper #1B: *Research Paper #1 labeled with the parts of a legal brief*

10. Library Research Paper #1B: *Library Research Paper #1 labeled with the parts of a legal brief*

Organization and Synthesis

1. Social Science MindMap (Point by Point)
2. Social Science MindMap (Block)

Chapter Three

Legal Writing from a Humanist's Perspective

*"The humanities, done right, are the crucible within which our evolving
notions of what it means to be fully human are put to the test; they teach
us, incrementally, endlessly, not what to do but how to be. Their method
is confrontational, their domain unlimited, their "product" not truth but
the reasoned search for truth, their "success" something very much like Frost's
momentary stay against confusion."*[24]

—Mark Slouka

Section 3-1: The Legal Memo— Legal Writing to Inform

The task of a humanist, a student of the humanities, is to understand and
communicate the artist's rendition of the human condition. A student of literature seeks to understand the writer's portrayal of life as it is, laying bare
emotion and making visible various perspectives of life's many facets. Students
of poetry and philosophy examine how poets and philosophers use words to
probe, express, and comprehend humanity's thoughts, feelings, and actions.
Students of dance, theatre, and film consider the use of the body and words
to recreate situations that show us ourselves as more vulnerable, beautiful,
fragile, and triumphant than we could imagine. Those who critically examine
the visual arts ponder how an artist creates from color, clay, and canvas reality and imagination. Students of music investigate how from silence the mu-

---

24. goodreads, http://www.goodreads.com/quotes/show_tag?name=humanities. This
is a reference to Robert Frost's essay, *The Figure a Poem Makes*, in which Frost describes a
poem as "a momentary stay against confusion," http://www.mrbauld.com/frostfig.html (last
visited Jul. 18, 2011).

sician brings form to sound and tells us a story that words are too simplistic to tell. The student of religion asks the enduring question of why, not because he or she desires to know why humans create but why humans were created. All of these disciplines, literature, philosophy, the visual and performing arts, and religion, make up the Humanities.[25]

Humanists communicate their examination of the human condition through analytical essays, exegetical and explicative essays, and argumentative papers/essays.

Section 3-2: Reading and Note-taking Strategies for Legal Authorities

Reading

In order to actively engage with the types of texts that humanists write, it is necessary to review the general structure of those common texts, their overall rhetorical purpose, and the rhetorical purpose of each of their parts.

Analytical Essay (Literature, Art, Dance, and Music)

A common type of writing in classes on visual and performing arts and literature is the analytical essay (*e.g.* criticism, interpretive essay, theoretical essay, etc.). To analyze is to consider the parts of a piece of art, music, or written work and examine the parts as they relate to the whole. An analytical essay is an examination of a piece of writing, music, or art (visual or performed) using a specified analytical framework to advance a thesis or argument. The rhetorical purpose of the analytical essay is to investigate the subject of the essay using the definition of its form or genre as an analytical framework, or by using the historical, political, economic, religious, and social context of its content and theories of the same. The author of an analytical essay may analyze according to form, genre, or theory separately or may utilize a combination of the three. The common structure of the analytical essay is as follows:[26]

---

25. *Please note:* History is also considered as part of the Humanities. In this book, it is treated as a Social Science. If you were taught history as a part of the Humanities, then this chapter will be more useful to you in understanding how writing in the Humanities translates to legal writing.

26. *See generally* Kennedy et al., *supra* note 20; Sylvan Barnet, A Short Guide to Writing About Art (6th ed. 2000); Jonathan D. Bellman, A Short Guide to Writ-

1. **Title:** *A detailed description of what the essay seeks to accomplish or about a particular piece or pieces of art, dance, music, or literature.*

2. **Introductory Paragraph:** *Provides the reader with a roadmap to the organizational structure of the piece or pieces used for analysis. Presents the thesis (the argument about the piece or pieces that the essay seeks to advance).*

3. **Supporting paragraphs:** *Compares and contrasts the similarities and differences in the various parts of a piece of art, music, or writing or in different pieces of art or writing in a manner that supports the thesis, all in the context of an analytical framework.*

4. **Conclusion:** *Offers an ending statement or statements that "answer" the thesis. Offers new observations about the subject or subjects of the analysis.*

5. **Works Cited:** *Gives attribution to any secondary sources used.*

Corresponding Parts of an Analytical Essay, Case, and Legal Memo

Parts of an Analytical Essay	Parts of a Case	Parts of a Legal Memo
Title	Case Name and Citation	"To, From, Date, Re" caption
Introductory Paragraph	Procedural Posture; Issue(s)	Question(s) Presented
Supporting Paragraphs	Facts; Synthesis of Legal Authorities; Factual Analysis	Statement of Facts; Discussion Section: Synthesis of Legal Authorities; Discussion Section: Factual Analysis
Conclusion	Ruling; Holding	Short Answer(s); Conclusion
Works Cited (*MLA, Chicago Manual of Style*)	*Bluebook* or *ALWD* citation form	*Bluebook* or *ALWD* citation form

MATERIALS: Two analytical essay examples are in the Reading and Note-taking folder located in the Exercises & Materials for this chapter as Analytical Essay #1: *Billy Pilgrim's Motion Sickness: Chronesthesia and*

ING ABOUT MUSIC (2d ed. 2007); and SYLVAN BARNET & WILLIAM E. CAIN, A SHORT GUIDE TO WRITING ABOUT LITERATURE (9th ed. 2003).

Duration in Slaughterhouse-Five; and Analytical Essay #2: *Hol(e)y Statues: Some reflections on holes, emptiness and longing in the work of two Australian émigré sculptors of the fifties.*

EXERCISE 1: Label Analytical Essay #1 or #2 by identifying the parts that correspond to the parts of a case and legal memo.

EXERCISE 2: Label one of the cases in the Legal Memo Case File with the parts that correspond to the parts of the analytical essay.

The Exegetical Essay (Philosophy and Religion)

Students of philosophy and religion often write exegeses or exegetical essays, which are critical interpretations or examinations of a written text and its other features (*i.e.* the author, historical context, grammatical structures, etc.). The subject of an exegesis, the text, can be a piece of philosophical writing or a scriptural passage. The rhetorical purpose of an exegesis is to extract meaning from the text to determine its significance in a broader context (*i.e.* historical, political, social, literary, biblical, philosophical, etc.). The basic structure of an exegetical essay is as follows:

1. **Title:** [*Names the subject of the exegesis; Gives a brief description of the subject of the exegesis.*]

2. **Introduction:** *Includes identification of [form], unit of thought [word, sentence, paragraph], atmosphere, and purpose. The purpose functions as the thesis of [the] paper.*

3. **Outline:** *Provide[s] an outline of [the passage selected].*

4. **Body:** *[Sets out the passage line-by-line or verse-by-verse and interweaves observations such as] word studies [which require secondary sources], textual analyses (if any) [which require secondary sources], background studies [which require secondary sources], and theological [or philosophical] implications [for the examined passage].*

5. **Conclusion:** *Reiterate[s] the purpose of the note [as well as] how [the] exegesis defends the larger purpose of the passage. Summarizes/synthesizes*

[the] theoretical implications and tie[s] them together for a final punch that points to the [deity or intellect/reasoning] revealed in the passage. Do[es] not include any application of the text.

6. **Works Cited:** *Include[s] proper APA or MLA standards [for] all works used.*[27]

Corresponding Parts of an Exegetical Essay, Case, and Legal Memo

Parts of an Exegetical Essay	Parts of a Case	Parts of a Legal Memo
Title	Case Name and Citation	"To, From, Date, Re" caption
Introduction	Procedural Posture; Issue(s)	Question(s) Presented
Outline	Facts	Statement of Facts
Body	Synthesis of Legal Authorities; Factual Analysis	Discussion Section: Synthesis of Legal Authorities; Discussion Section: Factual Analysis
Conclusion	Ruling; Holding	Short Answer(s); Conclusion
Works Cited *(APA, MLA, Chicago Manual of Style)*	*Bluebook* or *ALWD* citation form	*Bluebook* or *ALWD* citation form

MATERIALS: An example of an exegetical essay is in the Reading and Note-taking folder located in the Exercises & Materials for this chapter as Exegetical Essay #1: *'The Elijah who was to come': Matthew's use of Malachi (Matt 11:2–15).*

EXERCISE 3: Label Exegetical Essay #1 by identifying the parts that correspond to the parts of a case and legal memo.

EXERCISE 4: Label one of the cases in the Legal Memo Case File with the parts that correspond to the parts of the exegetical essay.

---

27. http://www.drurywriting.com (last visited Jul. 18, 2011).

The Explicative Essay (Literature)

The explicative essay, common in literature, is the brother of the exegetical essay. Unlike the exegetical essay, its primary rhetorical purpose is to reveal the meaning of a poem, play, or short piece of literature found in the form of the piece and from its actual verbiage, rather than viewing a piece of writing in a broader historical, social and/or political context. The common structure for an explicative essay is as follows:

1. **Title:** *Consists of the name of the piece used for explication, a more detailed description of what the explication seeks to accomplish, or an argument (thesis) about the purpose of the piece.*

2. **Introductory Paragraph:** *Provides the reader with a roadmap to the organizational structure of the piece used for explication. Also presents the thesis (argument) that the essay seeks to advance.*

3. **Supporting paragraphs:** *Follows the structure of the piece used for explication and provides explanations and descriptions of the text where appropriate.*[28] *Each paragraph advances the thesis.*

4. **Conclusion:** *Links argument to evidence and provides an ending statement that reinforces and answers the claims made in the opening paragraph.*[29]

5. **Works Cited:** *Gives attribution to the subject of the explication and any other sources used to bring meaning to the text.*

Corresponding Parts of an Explicative Essay, Case, and Legal Memo

Parts of an Explicative Essay	Parts of a Case	Parts of a Legal Memo
Title	Case Name and Citation	"To, From, Date, Re" caption
Introductory Paragraph	Procedural Posture; Issue(s)	Question(s) Presented
Supporting Paragraphs	Facts; Synthesis of Legal Authorities; Factual Analysis	Statement of Facts; Discussion Section: Synthesis of Legal Authorities; Discussion Section: Factual Analysis
Conclusion	Ruling; Holding	Short Answer(s); Conclusion
Works Cited (*APA, MLA, Chicago Manual of Style*)	*Bluebook* or *ALWD* citation form	*Bluebook* or *ALWD* citation form

---

28. BARNET & CAIN, *supra* note 26, at 44.
29. *Id.*

MATERIALS: Two examples of an explicative essay are in the Reading and Note-taking folder located in the Exercises & Materials for this chapter as Explicative Essay #1: *The Off-"Beat" Rhythms and Self-Expression in the Typography and Verse of Ntozake Shange*; and Explicative Essay #2: *John Donne's Via Media in 'Satire III'.*

EXERCISE 5: Label Explicative Essay #1 or #2 by identifying the parts that correspond to the parts of a case and legal memo.

EXERCISE 6: Label one of the cases in the Legal Memo Case File with the parts that correspond to the parts of the Explicative Essay #1 or #2.

The Argumentative Essay (Philosophy)

It is in the argumentative essay that the philosopher demonstrates an ability to answer a question posed about the human condition (*e.g. Should the death penalty be abolished?*) through logical (inductive or deductive) reasoning. The rhetorical purpose of the argumentative essay is to discuss a philosophical proposition by investigating claims (arguments, factual assertions) made for and against it, and the warrants (reasons) supporting those claims. The basic structure of an argumentative essay is as follows:

1. Title: *A description of the subject of the paper or what the paper seeks to accomplish.*

2. Introduction: *Defines the subject of the question using the work of philosophers and other secondary sources.*

3. Supporting Paragraphs: *Discuss the reasons for (arguments) and against (counter-arguments) the query in the Introduction and the assumptions that underlie those reasons; illustrate each argument using relevant examples.*

4. Conclusion: *Offers an answer to the query posed in the Introduction after a careful consideration of the arguments and counter-arguments.*

5. **Works Cited:** *Gives attribution to the secondary sources used in the paper.*

Corresponding Parts of an Argumentative Essay, Case, and Legal Memo

Parts of an Argumentative Essay	Parts of a Case	Parts of a Legal Memo
Title	Case Name and Citation	"To, From, Date, Re" caption
Introduction	Procedural Posture; Issue(s)	Question(s) Presented
Supporting Paragraphs	Synthesis of Legal Authorities; Factual Analysis	Discussion Section: Synthesis of Legal Authorities; Discussion Section: Factual Analysis
Conclusion	Ruling; Holding	Short Answer(s); Conclusion
Works Cited *(APA, MLA, Chicago Manual of Style)*	*Bluebook* or *ALWD* citation form	*Bluebook* or *ALWD* citation form

MATERIALS: An example of an argumentative essay is in the Reading and Note-taking folder located in the Exercises & Materials for this chapter as Argumentative Essay #1: *Get Your Paws Off of My Pixels: Personal Identity and Avatars as Self.*

EXERCISE 7: Label Argumentative Essay #1 with the parts that correspond to the parts of a case and legal memo.

EXERCISE 8: Label one of the cases in the Legal Memo Case File with the parts that correspond to the parts of the argumentative essay.

Note-taking

Exegetical and Explicative Essays

Exegetical and explicative essays are instructive for how closely cases must be read. The amount of time and attention that the author of these essays spends in examining a line or a passage is equivalent to the care that a lawyer must spend examining the words, lines, and paragraphs in a case for the purpose of case briefing and note-taking.

In writing an exegetical or explicative essay, the writer is not only concerned with what the words and sentences in a passage mean but also with the relationship of the sentences to each other and the relationship of a passage in relationship to others. These micro considerations (words, sentences and passages) and macro considerations (the relationship between words, sentences, and passages) help the reader to make meaning of the work as a whole. The legal reader has the same goal in examining the parts of a case and the relationship between its parts (citation, procedural posture, facts, *ratio decidendi*, and ruling) to determine its holding, the meaning of the case. After determining the meaning of the case, the legal reader takes the extra step to explore how the case (its facts and holding) are similar to or dissimilar to the facts of their client's case. The lawyer determines the meaning of a case through critical reading and case briefing. The lawyer determines the significance of the case, the implications that the case has for their client, through note-taking.

Corresponding Parts of an Exegetical Essay and Case Brief

Parts of an Exegetical Essay	Parts of a Case Brief
Title	Case Name and Citation
Introduction	Procedural Posture; Issue(s)
Outline	Facts
Body	*Ratio Decidendi*: Synthesis of Legal Authorities (Rule); *Ratio Decidendi*: Factual Analysis
Conclusion	Ruling; Holding
Works Cited *(APA, MLA, Chicago Manual of Style)*	*Bluebook* or *ALWD* citation form

Corresponding Parts of an Explicative Essay and Case Brief

Parts of an Explicative Essay	Parts of a Case Brief
Title	Case Name and Citation
Introductory Paragraph	Procedural Posture; Issue(s)
Supporting Paragraphs	Facts; *Ratio Decidendi*: Synthesis of Legal Authorities (Rule); *Ratio Decidendi*: Factual Analysis
Conclusion	Ruling, Holding
Works Cited *(APA, MLA, Chicago Manual of Style)*	*Bluebook* or *ALWD* citation form

---

EXERCISE 9: Revisit Exegetical Essay #1 and Explicative Essay #1. Review how the author explains the relationship between the words, sentences and passages. After you have done so, complete Exercises 4, 5, and 6 in Chapter 1.

Analytical Essays

When reading secondary sources to help develop an analytical essay or an argumentative essay, students of the Humanities ask themselves the following questions:

1. What is the topic of the reading? *(The topic is the overall theme of the reading.)*

2. What is the subject of the reading? *(The piece of art, music, or literature about which the author is writing.)*

3. What is the author's thesis? *(The focus of the essay or paper, and the main argument that the author wishes to make.)*

4. What support does the author give for the thesis?

5. Are the sources of support adequate? Why or why not?

6. What kind of conclusions does the author make in the paper?

7. Did the author adequately support the thesis?

8. After completing the reading, what have I learned? What new insights have I gained?

These questions allow the reader to determine the major category or categories in which the text falls (formal analysis or theoretical analysis, for example); ascertain the major concepts within the category or categories that the author explores (different forms and their characteristics or a specific type of criticism and its characteristics); and to evaluate whether the author has adequately explored the concepts and supported any assertions made about the concepts. In examining the major category or categories in which the text falls and the major concepts in those categories, the reader determines the meaning(s) ascribed to the subject of the writing. In deciding whether the author has adequately explored the concepts and supported any assertions made about the concepts, the reader determines the implications of the author's assertions for the subject of the writing. Again, this is similar to the lawyer's work in that a lawyer determines the meaning of a case through critical reading and case briefing. The lawyer determines the significance of the case, the implications that the case has for their client, through note-taking.

Reading Questions and their Case Brief Counterparts

Reading Questions	Parts of a Case Brief
What is the topic of the reading?	Procedural Posture
What is the subject of the reading?	Facts
What is the author's thesis?	Issue(s)
What support does the author give for the thesis? Are the sources of support adequate? Why or why not?	*Ratio Decidendi*: Synthesis of Legal Authorities (Rule)
Did the author adequately support the thesis?	*Ratio Decidendi*: Factual Analysis
What kinds of conclusions does the author make?	Ruling
After completing the reading, what have I learned? What new insight have I gained?	Holding

Complete **EXERCISES 4, 5**, and **6** in Chapter 1.

Section 3-3: Organizing and Synthesizing Legal Authorities

When humanists write the supporting paragraphs of an analytical essay or argumentative essay and the body of an exegetical essay, they must synthesize relevant secondary sources to help them build a framework for analysis. If the humanist is conducting a formal analysis, the requirements and characteristics of the form or style itself (sculpture, ballet, sonata, binary, ternary) become the framework to analyze how the subject of the analysis (the piece of music, artwork, or dance) conforms to the form, deviates from it, and why. If the humanist is engaging in a theoretical analysis, an analysis that views the subject in its social, political, economical, and/or historical context, then the particular theory or theories relevant to each (feminist theory, Marxist theory, etc.) become the framework for analysis. Using the theoretical framework, the humanist decides which aspects of the theory are relevant to the subject, which are not, and why. Likewise, the author of an argumentative essay must synthesize secondary sources to both comprehend and define the subject of the question for analysis and then support the assertions and reasons that they will make in answering the question.

The type of analysis that a humanist undertakes in large measure determines the organizational structure for the synthesis. While there are several main types of organizational schemes,[30] the type that most closely resembles a legal synthesis of authorities is the structure of comparison and contrast. In using comparison and contrast as an analytical tool, the humanist may consult sources as to form, characteristics or theoretical frameworks and then compare and contrast them to the subject of the analysis.

Although the legal writer also uses the analytical tool of comparison and contrast in developing a synthesis of authorities, the manner in which the legal writer uses comparison and contrast differs from how the humanist uses them in two important ways. First, the humanist may or may not make explicit definitions of form or theory in the text but rather assume that the reader already has knowledge of them. This is especially true in formal analyses, which are written for an audience who already has an operating knowledge of the form. Second, humanists interweave theories and definitions throughout the text of the

---

30. *See* KENNEDY ET AL., *supra* note 20, at 486–487. Other organizational structures mentioned are organization by proposition and organization by the cause-and-effect relationships among sources.

essay as they simultaneously discuss the subject of the essay. Legal writers, on the other hand, place the whole of the synthesis of legal authorities before any analysis of the facts of their client's case. In doing so, they make the analytical framework explicit. The reason for these two different approaches rests in the rhetorical purposes for both types of writing. Ultimately, any analysis a humanist performs on a text places primacy on the text. The humanist text is parallel (or comparable) to the facts of a client's case in the legal arena. The rhetorical purpose of the legal memo is not to place primacy on the facts of the case, but rather the precedent that allows the lawyer to interpret the facts of the client's case.

EXERCISE 10: For Analytical Essay #1, Exegetical Essay #1, and Argumentative Essay #1, each respectively, identify if it is a formal or theoretical analysis and note the organizational structure of each. Next, highlight in the text where the author explicitly uses a source of information about theory or form as the framework for analysis and where the author implicitly uses such information as a framework for analysis. After you have completed Exercise 8 in Chapter 1, note the similarities and differences in how the humanist and legal writer use comparison and contrast.

A Note on Argumentative Papers/Essays

Comparisons and contrasts for argumentative essays are usually organized in a point-by-point or block format.[31] Under the point-by-point structure, the author separates the essay into categories and then within each category lists the major concepts. For each of the sources relevant to a particular concept, the writer explains the similarities and differences between them. In explaining the differences between the authorities, the author summarizes, paraphrases, and quotes them.

---

31. *Id.* at 83–86, 96–100.

Outline of a Comparison and Contrast Organized Point by Point

Topic: Assisted Suicide

Question: Should assisted suicide be legalized to allow the sick and the elderly to end their lives when they desire?

Authorities Used: Hatfield and McCoy

Introduction

I. The Value of Human Life (CATEGORY 1)

    A. The State's Responsibility to the Sick and Elderly (CONCEPT A)—What does each author say about this concept? What are the similarities and differences between each author's assertions?

    B. The Physician's Responsibility to the Sick and Elderly (CONCEPT B)—What does each author say about this concept? What are the similarities and differences between each author's assertions?

    C. Society's Responsibility to the Sick and Elderly—(CONCEPT C)—What does each author say about this concept? What are the similarities and differences between each author's assertions?

II. Availability of Healthcare (CATEGORY 2)

    A. The State's Responsibility to the Sick and Elderly (CONCEPT A)—What does each author say about the concept? What are the similarities and differences between each author's assertions?

    B. The Physician's Responsibility to the Sick and Elderly (CONCEPT B)—What does each author say about the concept? What are the similarities and differences between each author's assertions?

    C. Society's Responsibility to the Sick and Elderly (CONCEPT C)—What does each author say about the concept? What are the similarities and differences between each author's assertions?

For the block structure, the author first separates the essay by the number of relevant sources. Under each source, the author further separates the essay into the categories that each source discusses, and then by the concepts within those categories. In the block structure, the author discusses the sources in turn, explaining the differences in the categories and concepts as the essay progresses. The author's explanation of the similarities and differences between the sources requires summaries, paraphrases, and quotations from them.

Outline of a Comparison and Contrast Organized by Block

Topic: Assisted Suicide

Question: Should assisted suicide be legalized to allow the sick and the elderly to end their lives when they desire?

Authorities Used: Hatfield and McCoy

Introduction

I. Hatfield

    A. The Value of Human Life (CATEGORY 1)

        1. The State's Responsibility to the Sick and Elderly (CONCEPT A)

        2. The Physician's Responsibility to the Sick and Elderly (CONCEPT B)

        3. Society's Responsibility to the Sick and Elderly—(CONCEPT C)

    B. Availability of Healthcare (CATEGORY 2)

        1. The State's Responsibility to the Sick and Elderly (CONCEPT A)

        2. The Physician's Responsibility to the Sick and Elderly (CONCEPT B)

        3. Society's Responsibility to the Sick and Elderly (CONCEPT C)

II. McCoy

    A. The Value of Human Life (CATEGORY 1)

        1. The State's Responsibility to the Sick and Elderly (CONCEPT A)

        2. The Physician's Responsibility to the Sick and Elderly (CONCEPT B)

        3. Society's Responsibility to the Sick and Elderly—(CONCEPT C)

    B. Availability of Healthcare (CATEGORY 2)

        1. The State's Responsibility to the Sick and Elderly (CONCEPT A)

        2. The Physician's Responsibility to the Sick and Elderly (CONCEPT B)

        3. Society's Responsibility to the Sick and Elderly (CONCEPT C)

MATERIALS: Examples of the point-by-point and block outlines above in MindMap form are in the Organization and Synthesis folder located in the Exercises & Materials for this chapter.

EXERCISE 11: Outline or MindMap the structure of Argumentative Essay #1. Is it organized point by point or by block? What are the assertions that the writer makes in the essay? What are the reasons that support each assertion? Are the reasons and assertions ordered inductively or deductively?

Complete **EXERCISES 7** and **8** in Chapter 1.

Section 3-4: Using Legal Authorities to Analyze Facts and to Develop Conclusions

Analysis

Regardless of how comparison and contrast are used, the uses detailed above require the humanist and legal writer to make assertions and to support those assertions with reasons. The assertions are guided by the thesis of the essay; each assertion (in the form of a topic sentence or concluding sentence of a paragraph) must advance the thesis, each sentence in the paragraph must support the topic sentence, and each paragraph must progress the reader toward the thesis in a logical manner. The main difference between how a legal writer conducts analysis and how the humanist does lies in how it appears in the writing. Again, a humanist interweaves synthesis and analysis throughout the essay, noting how a source interprets the subject of an analysis while simultaneously giving examples to support the observation. The legal writer presents the analysis after developing the framework for analysis in the synthesis of legal authorities. The interweaving that the legal writer does in the analysis seeks to discuss the facts of their client's case in the language of the rule synthesis, and to provide factual illustrations or analogies from the authorities in the synthesis to provide support for assertions when necessary, relevant, and directly applicable.

> **EXERCISE 12:** Using any of the essay examples in the Reading and Note-taking folder for this chapter, highlight in the text where the author uses the subject of the analysis to provide support for their assertions. After you have completed Exercise 9 in Chapter 1, note the similarities and differences in how the humanist and legal writer use comparison and contrast to analyze the subject of the analysis.

> Complete **EXERCISES 9** and **10** in Chapter 1.

Developing Conclusions

Unlike lawyers, humanists are not always looking for absolute answers in interpreting pieces of music, artwork, or dance or interested in answering philosophical questions concretely and definitively. However, both types of writers are concerned with whether the subject of the analysis has met the criteria for interpretation or not and how. The author of a legal memo follows the analytical process to a final conclusion that thoroughly discusses how the criteria for evaluation have or have not been met.

> **PUTTING IT ALL TOGETHER:**
> Using the skills that you have learned for building a legal memo, complete the legal memo assignment for the case file assigned to you.

Section 3-5: The Legal Brief— Writing to Persuade

Before beginning to read this section, review the Legal Brief Case File in the Exercises & Materials for Chapter One.

Complete **EXERCISES 11** and **12** in Chapter 1.

Organization

As discussed previously, the main goal of the humanist is to understand and communicate the human condition. The various ways that a humanist does this is through the analytical essay, exegetical or explicative essay, and the argumentative paper/essay. None of these types of writing is purely objective or for informational purposes only. Rather, the overarching rhetorical purpose of all, except the argumentative essay, is to advance a particular reading of a text. In examining the structure of the different types of writing in the humanities, we noted how the authors made assertions and supported those assertions with reasons in a manner that advanced a particular thesis. This is the essence of persuasive writing. For any of the essay examples in this chapter, note how the topic sentences or main assertions of each paragraph support the thesis and how the support for each topic sentence/assertion is a reference to the text itself or a secondary source that supports a particular reading of the text in line with the author's thesis. The topic sentences/assertions in each paragraph function similarly to point headings in a legal brief. The author's usage of secondary sources and textual examples are like the persuasive synthesis of authorities and persuasive analysis in the argument portion of the legal brief. Review the answers to Exercises 1, 3, 5, and 7 in this chapter to see the relationship between topic sentences/assertions, secondary sources, and textual examples in a piece of writing.

The parts of the analytical essay, exegetical or explicative essay, and the argumentative essay correspond to the parts of the legal brief as follows:

Parts of an Analytical Essay	Parts of the Legal Brief
Title	Notice of Motion or Cover Sheet
Introductory Paragraph	Introduction; Motion Standard of Review; Statement of Facts
Supporting Paragraphs	Argument: Persuasive Rule Synthesis; Argument: Factual Analysis/Argument
Conclusion	Conclusion
Works Cited	Table of Authorities (*if included*)

EXERCISE 13: Label Analytical Essay #1: *Billy Pilgrim's Motion Sickness: Chronesthesia and Duration in Slaughterhouse-Five* or Analytical Essay #2: *Hol(e)y Statues: Some reflections on holes, emptiness and longing in the work of two Australian émigré sculptors of the fifties* by identifying the parts that correspond to the parts of a legal brief.

Parts of an Exegetical Essay	Parts of the Legal Brief
Title	Notice of Motion or Cover Sheet
Introduction	Introduction; Motion Standard of Review
Outline	Statement of Facts
Body	Argument: Persuasive Rule Synthesis; Argument: Factual Analysis/Argument
Conclusion	Conclusion
Works Cited	Table of Authorities (*if included*)

EXERCISE 14: Label Exegetical Essay #1: *'The Elijah who was to come': Matthew's use of Malachi (Matt 11:2–15)* by identifying the parts that correspond to the parts of a legal brief.

Parts of an Explicative Essay	Parts of the Legal Brief
Title	Notice of Motion or Cover Sheet
Introductory Paragraph	Introduction; Motion Standard of Review; Statement of Facts
Supporting Paragraphs	Argument: Persuasive Rule Synthesis; Argument: Factual Analysis/Argument
Conclusion	Conclusion
Works Cited	Table of Authorities *(if included)*

EXERCISE 15: Label Explicative Essay #1: *The Off-"Beat" Rhythms and Self-Expression in the Typography and Verse of Ntozake Shange* or Explicative Essay #2: *John Donne's Via Media in 'Satire III'* by identifying the parts that correspond to the parts of a legal brief.

Parts of an Argumentative Essay	Parts of the Legal Brief
Title	Notice of Motion or Cover Sheet
Introduction	Introduction; Motion Standard of Review; Statement of Facts
Supporting Paragraphs	Argument: Persuasive Rule Synthesis; Argument: Factual Analysis/Argument
Conclusion	Conclusion
Works Cited	Table of Authorities *(if included)*

EXERCISE 16: Label Argumentative Essay #1: *Get Your Paws Off of My Pixels: Personal Identity and Avatars as Self* by identifying the parts that correspond to the parts of a legal brief.

Complete **EXERCISE 13** in Chapter 1.

Synthesis

In synthesizing sources for use in humanities writing, a humanist must engage with previous authors who have covered the same or similar subjects. In engaging with these authors, the humanist must anticipate the multiple ways that texts (both the subject of the analysis and writings about that subject) can be read and, during the writing process, focus the texts to emphasize the portions that support the thesis or de-emphasize the portions that do not. The author may emphasize key portions of a text by placing summaries, paraphrases, or quotes of it in prominent places or by repeating key phrases in the text that directly support the thesis. During this process, the author must decide how to explain portions of a text that run contrary to their thesis in a manner that does not undermine their thesis. Please review any of the essay examples for this chapter for how the author engages with various texts to develop a persuasive framework for their thesis.

Complete **EXERCISE 14** in Chapter 1.

Analysis and Conclusions

When a humanist analyzes a text in an analytical essay, they generally use either the form of the text or theory as a framework to assess the strengths and weaknesses of certain readings of the text as advocated by the thesis. In constructing an argumentative essay, the philosopher does the same but mainly to assess the strengths and weaknesses of a particular argument or line of reasoning. As discussed previously, the humanist must support the thesis through assertions and reasons based in the form and/or theory, and primarily by using relevant examples from the text, the subject of the analysis. Just as the writers in the essay examples decided how to emphasize and de-emphasize the text or other types of writing about it in the synthesis, they also decided how to emphasize examples from the text that supported their theses and de-emphasize those that did not. Review any of the essay examples for this chapter to determine how the author uses examples from the text when interpreting it in a manner consistent with the thesis.

A Note About Argumentative Essays

Typically, assertions and reasons in argumentative essays are ordered inductively (reasons follow assertions) or deductively (reasons lead to assertions).

In this regard, the structure and content of the argumentative essay most closely mimics the structure and content of the legal brief.

> Complete **EXERCISES 15** and **16** in Chapter 1.

> **PUTTING IT ALL TOGETHER:**
> *Using the skills that you have learned for constructing a legal brief, complete the legal brief assignment for the case file assigned to you.*

Section 3-6: Exercises & Materials List

This section corresponds to the Exercises & Materials folder located on the CD-ROM that accompanies this text. The following folders and their contents are located within the Exercises & Materials folder for this chapter:

Reading and Note-taking

1. Analytical Essay #1: *Billy Pilgrim's Motion Sickness: Chronesthesia and Duration in Slaughterhouse-Five*

2. Analytical Essay #2: *Hol(e)y Statues: Some reflections on holes, emptiness and longing in the work of two Australian émigré sculptors of the fifties.*

3. Exegetical Essay #1: *'The Elijah who was to come': Matthew's use of Malachi (Matt 11:2–15)*

4. Explicative Essay #1: *The Off-"Beat" Rhythms and Self-Expression in the Typography and Verse of Ntozake Shange*

5. Explicative Essay #2: *John Donne's Via Media in 'Satire III'*

6. Argumentative Essay #1: *Get Your Paws Off of My Pixels: Personal Identity and Avatars as Self*

Organization and Synthesis

1. Humanities MindMap (Point by Point)

2. Humanities MindMap (Block)

Chapter Four

Legal Writing from an Artist's Perspective

"The medium is the message."[32]

—Marshall McLuhan

Section 4-1: The Legal Memo — Legal Writing to Inform

The artist creates, and by doing so seeks to understand and communicate the human condition. A writer of literature seeks to portray life as it is, laying bare emotion and making visible various perspectives of life's many facets. The poet and playwright use words to probe, express, and comprehend humanity's thoughts, feelings and actions. The dancer, choreographer, and actor use the body and words to recreate situations that show us ourselves as more vulnerable, beautiful, fragile, and triumphant than we could imagine. The artist creates reality and imagination from color, clay, and canvas. From silence, the musician and composer bring form to sound and tell us a story that words are too simplistic to tell. This collection of disciplines, art, music, and dance, and all that they encompass are known as The Arts. The rhetorical purpose of art is simple: "Art is the shaping of some material to provide an aesthetic experience."[33]

---

32. MARSHALL McLUHAN, UNDERSTANDING MEDIA: THE EXTENSIONS OF MAN 7 (1964).
33. JACQUELINE SMITH, DANCE COMPOSITION — A PRACTICAL GUIDE FOR TEACHERS 14 (1976).

Section 4-2: Reading and Note-taking Strategies for Legal Authorities

Art originates as a concept, which is subsequently expressed in the form of the idea. The act of "reading art" for the artist, then, is the act of seeking inspiration for concepts or assimilating expressions of concepts (ideas) that are similar to what the artist desires to express. In gathering inspiration for a painting, a painter may take a trip to a local museum or browse collections of paintings in a book. A composer may read a poem and then listen to pieces that express poems as music, with or without words, to learn different techniques for doing the same. The choreographer may consider the sounds of the city or the way a flower bends in the wind in choreographing a dance. Unlike the methodical deconstruction of a case, legal memo, or legal brief that a lawyer undertakes to determine how to recreate each piece of written work, the deconstruction of art for the purpose of creating it is a less certain proposition. The artist finds ideas and inspiration from an unlimited number of sources. In attempting to determine what art "means" or what it is attempting to say, it is possible for the knowledgeable viewer or listener to determine form, deviations from form, and other influences that the artist uses to create a particular piece and express an idea. However, the act of creation itself necessitates departure from a strict reproduction of what is seen and heard.

This is not to say that an artist creates without the help of guiding principles, rules, and techniques. On the contrary, the elements of art (its raw materials), the way they are arranged (forms, genres/styles), and the techniques in arranging them are integral to the creative process. They are as follows:

Art (*Visual*)

The elements of art are the building blocks of art, much like cases are the building blocks for a legal memo.

Elements of Art[34]

· Line	· Space	· Shape
· Color		· Texture

---

34. Marjorie Elliot Bevlin, Design Through Discovery: An Introduction to Art and Design 45–122 (6th ed. 1993).

The genres, styles, and forms of art correspond to the synthesis of legal authorities in both a case and legal memo. The execution of the genre/style and form is equivalent to the analysis sections of both.

Common Art Genres/Styles[35]

- Impressionism
- Expressionism
- Abstraction
- Cubism
- Surrealism

Common Art Types/Forms

- Painting
- Drawing
- Sculpture
- Graphics
- Printmaking
- Ceramics

The techniques in art correspond to the rhetorical moves that a legal writer makes in crafting both the synthesis and analysis portions of a case and legal memo.

Examples of Art Techniques[36]

- Hammering (Metal)
- Welding (Sculpture)
- Glassblowing
- Coiling (Clay)
- Weaving (Fibers/Textiles)
- Spinning (Metal)
- Casting (Sculpture)
- Pinching (Clay)
- Throwing (Clay)
- Fresco (Painting)

EXERCISE 1: Revisit a piece of artwork that you have created. List its genre/style, form, and any of the different techniques that you used to craft the piece.

---

35. *Id.* at 230.
36. *Id.* at 211–230.

Music

The elements of music are the building blocks of music, much like cases are the building blocks for a legal memo.

Elements of Music[37]

- Melody
- Rhythm
- Dynamics
- Harmony
- Form
- Texture
- Timbre

The genres, styles, and forms of music correspond to the synthesis of legal authorities in both a case and legal memo. The execution of the genre/style and form is equivalent to the analysis sections of both.

Common Music Genres/Styles

- Classical
- Jazz
- Dance
- Blues
- Gospel
- Pop
- Rhythm and Blues

Common Music Forms[38]

- Binary (A B)/Ternary (A B A)
- Rondo (A B A C A D A)
- Sonata
- Blues[39]
- Verse—Chorus[40]

Music compositional techniques correspond to the rhetorical moves that a legal writer makes in crafting both the synthesis and analysis portions of a case and legal memo.

---

37. MARK EVAN BONDS, LISTEN TO THIS 1–14 (2d ed. 2010).

38. STEFAN KOSTKA & DOROTHY PAYNE, TONAL HARMONY 335–342 *(binary/ternary)*, 344–354 *(sonata)*, 354–358 *(rondo)* (6th ed. 2008).

39. BONDS, *supra* note 37, at 393; KOSTKA & PAYNE, *supra* note 38, at 343.

40. BONDS, *supra* note 37, at 477.

Examples of Music Compositional Techniques

- Change of Mode and Modal Mixture[41]
- Motivic Development/Thematic Metamorphosis[42]
- Polytonality and Bi-Tonality[43]
- Serialism/Twelve-Tone Technique[44]
- Instrumentation and Orchestration[45]
- Cannon and other Contrapuntal Techniques[46]

EXERCISE 2: Revisit a piece of music that you composed. List its genre/style, form, and any compositional techniques that you used to create the piece.

Dance

The elements of dance are the building blocks of dance, much like cases are the building blocks for a legal memo.

Elements of Dance[47]

•Movement	• Time
• Space	• Force/Energy
• Form	

The genres, styles, and forms of dance correspond to the synthesis of legal authorities in both a case and legal memo. The execution of the genre/style and/or form is equivalent to the analysis sections of both.

---

41. Leon Dallin, Techniques of Twentieth Century Composition: A Guide to the Materials of Modern Music 104–121 (3d ed. 1974).
    42. *Id.* at 166–177.
    43. *Id.* at 123–136.
    44. *Id.* at 189–207.
    45. *See generally* Samuel Adler, The Study of Orchestration (3d ed. 2002).
    46. *See generally* Kent Kennan, Counterpoint (4th ed. 1998).
    47. Smith, *supra* note 33, at 25, 70.

Common Dance Genres/Styles

- Ballet
- Jazz
- Hip-Hop
- Swing
- Country & Western

- Tap
- Modern
- Folk
- Ballroom
- Latin

Common Dance Forms[48]

- Binary (A B)
- Rondo (A B A C A D A)
- Canon or Fugue

- Ternary (A B A)
- Theme and Variation
- Narrative Form

The choreographic devices in dance correspond to the rhetorical moves that a legal writer makes in crafting both the synthesis and analysis portions of a case and legal memo.

Examples of Dance Choreographic Devices[49]

- Cannon
- Unison
- Repetition
- Call and Response (Question and Answer)
- Counterpoint
- Mirroring (Copying)
- Interweaving Patterns
- Spatial Design

EXERCISE 3: Revisit a favorite dance performance that you choreographed. List its genre/style, form, and any choreographic devices that you used in developing the piece.

---

48. *Id.* at 72–75.
49. *Id.* at 56–67.

Complete **EXERCISES 3**, **4**, **5** and **6** in Chapter 1.
Note: For more discipline-specific examples of reading and note-taking, review Section 3-2 in Chapter 3 (Legal Writing from a Humanitarian's Perspective).

Section 4-3: Organizing and Synthesizing Legal Authorities

After expressing a concept as an idea for a piece of art, the artist develops an idea according to a plan. The plan for the piece can be shaped by external constraints, such as the amount of money available for the project, the number of performers needed, the size of the gallery or performance space, and/or available materials. Various artistic forms can also shape the plan. The plan may only be shaped by an idea. Regardless, external factors and formal factors provide an organizational structure for the development of an artistic idea, much like how the concepts and categories pulled from the cases form the structure for the synthesis of legal authorities. In developing music, dance, or art, the artist must assemble the raw materials of the art form into a structure that serves the overall purpose and intention of the piece given the available resources. The legal writer does the same when synthesizing legal authorities; the process requires assembling the concepts in the authorities according to categories in a manner that assesses and resolves a client's problems.

EXERCISE 4: Note the genres/style, form, artistic technique(s), compositional technique(s) or choreographic technique(s) used in any of the pieces that you revisited above. How did you arrange the basic elements required for the art form according to idea, style/genre, form, technique/device and/or external factors (if observable)? If you used a specific form or style/genre to organize the piece did you follow it strictly or did you deviate from it? If you deviated from it, how did you do so? Write down your answers to these questions in the form of a MindMap or outline.

Complete **EXERCISE 7** in Chapter 1.

Legal authorities are synthesized when combined into words, phrases, sentences, and paragraphs according to category and concept for the purpose of resolving a legal issue or answering a *Question Presented*. Like a legal synthesis, a piece of art, dance, or music composition is "drafted" (composed or choreographed) using the equivalent of words, phrases, sentences, and paragraphs arranged to convey an idea. In dance, the way movements or movement patterns are arranged to express parts of the overarching idea of the piece is called a "motif" or "motive." These are the functional equivalents of words. The stringing together of motifs using different choreographic devices is called a "phrase." The "sentence" is a further development of the phrase, and the sum of the sentences is the equivalent of a paragraph. Each paragraph advances the overall idea of the piece by further developing the original motif or introducing a new one to develop.[50] The overall idea is similar to the legal issues in a case or the *Question(s) Presented* in a legal memo.

In music, notes are the equivalent of letters in written work. The way that the notes are arranged to express parts of the overarching idea of the piece is called a "motif" or "motive."[51] The stringing together of motives using various compositional techniques is called a "phrase."[52] The "sentence" is a completion of a musical phrase (a full expression of an idea), and the sum of the sentences, a "section," is the equivalent of a paragraph. Each section advances the overall idea or theme of the composition by further developing the original motive or introducing a new one to develop.

A motif in art is usually refers to a recurring unit that creates a pattern. While this concept captures some of the parallels between developing art and drafting a legal memo, it does not fully articulate them. The artist begins with a concept and the goal of the artwork, the finished product, is a realization of that concept.[53] In this sense, the concept is akin to a word. The artist's expression of the concept through shapes, lines, colors, and textures equal phrases and sentences, and the arrangement of those shapes, lines, colors and textures in space (two or three dimensional space) equal paragraphs. Each new layer of arrangement further develops the concept until the piece is finished.

---

50. Russell Meriwether Hughes, Dance Composition: The Basic Elements 41 (1965); Smith, *supra* note 33, at 40–43.

51. Don Michael Randel, The New Harvard Dictionary of Music 513 (2d ed. 1986).

52. *Id.* at 629.

53. Bevlin, *supra* note 34, at 28.

EXERCISE 5: For the pieces that you created above, observe their compositional equivalents to words, phrases, sentences, and paragraphs. After you have done so, review the table below to see the corresponding parts of your art, dance or music composition to the rhetorical moves needed to draft the rule synthesis.

Corresponding Parts of Pieces of Art, Music or Dance and Rhetorical Moves for Drafting a Rule Synthesis

Rhetorical Moves	Music	Dance	Art
Determine the cause of action	Motive/Motif	Motive/Motif	Concept
Categorize the authorities according to the questions that you want answered OR the issues that you want to explore within the cause of action; Define the category and its concepts	Phrase	Phrase	Expression through shape, line, color, and texture
Compare and contrast the similarities and differences between the authorities using the major concepts in the authorities organized by category	Sentence	Sentence	Arrangement of shape, line, color, and texture in space
Explain those similarities and differences in turn and how they impact your understanding of the relationship between authorities for the major concepts in each category; Connect all of the explanations moving from concept to concept, category to category until all of the legal authority is exhausted	Section	Paragraph	Development to the finished piece

Complete **EXERCISE 8** in Chapter 1.

Section 4-4: Using Legal Authorities to Analyze Facts and to Develop Conclusions

Analysis

The analysis part of creating a dance, piece of music, or work of art is an exercise in trial and error. It is here that the artist tests possible executions of the idea and tweaks them to conform to the original vision. During this process, the artist will be concerned with the functionality of the finished work, its development in terms of external constraints, and its ability to express the artist's concepts or ideas. Legal writing progresses through a similar process in the analysis portion of the memo, as the analysis is the expression of the synthesis of legal authorities using the facts of the case.

> **EXERCISE 6:** Think back to the time when you created the piece of art that you examined above? Did you have problems with its functionality? Developing it in terms of any external constraints? If so, how did you address these problems? How did you polish the piece to conform to your overall idea?

> Complete **EXERCISES 9** and **10** in Chapter 1.

Developing Conclusions

The artistic equivalent of a legal conclusion is the completion of the work itself. Completion may include a public aspect, such as a dance or music performance or an art showing. It may also be private, the quiet satisfaction of executing an idea. Regardless, like its counterpart in the legal memo, it is both an ending and a beginning; it is the end point to the artist's expression and simultaneously the beginning of an audience's interpretation of the work. The legal conclusion presents a likely resolution to the client's dilemma but also is an entrée into additional work that may be completed on a client's behalf (*e.g.* drafting a legal brief).

PUTTING IT ALL TOGETHER:
Using the skills that you have learned for building a legal memo, complete the legal memo assignment for the case file assigned to you.

Section 4-5: The Legal Brief— Writing to Persuade

Before beginning to read this section, review the Legal Brief Case File in the Exercises & Materials for Chapter One.

Complete **EXERCISES 11** and **12** in Chapter 1.

As we discussed before, the rhetorical purpose of art is to shape material for an aesthetic purpose.[54] The artist achieves this through the process of creating, as well as in the act or process of creation. The artist's intent is to convey an idea or emotion and to engage the senses. From this perspective, a work of art's persuasive value lies in its ability to actually convey the artist's intent. In the same way, a legal brief's persuasive value lies in the author's ability to convince the judge to view the case and all of its possible resolutions from the client's point of view.

If you review Sections 4-1, 4-2, 4-3, and 4-4 you will find that the same instruction holds true for the legal brief. The elements of art, dance, and music are the building blocks for these art forms like cases are the building blocks for the legal brief. The genres/styles and forms/types of the arts and their execution are the equivalent of the persuasive synthesis of authorities and analysis/argument parts of the legal brief, respectively. The main difference between the legal memo/legal brief from an artistic perspective is intentionality. The choreographer, composer, and artist arrange the raw material of their art form for the purposes of expressing their idea or perspective. The legal brief writer

---

54. Smith, *supra* note 33, at 14.

arranges the building blocks of the legal brief with the intention of presenting the case and its possible resolutions from the client's perspective.

Complete **EXERCISES 13**, **14**, **15** and **16** in Chapter 1.

PUTTING IT ALL TOGETHER:
Using the skills that you have learned for constructing a legal brief, complete the legal brief assignment in the case file assigned to you.

Section 4-6: Exercises & Materials List

Review the Exercises & Materials for *Chapter Three: Legal Writing from a Humanitarian's Perspective*.

Chapter Five

Legal Writing from a Scientist's Perspective

"[S]cience is not a collection of facts. It is the organization of the facts under general laws, and the laws in turn are all held together by such concepts, such creations of the human mind, as gravitation. The facts are endless chaos [...] science is the human activity of finding an order in nature by organizing the scattered, meaningless facts under universal concepts."[55]

—Jacob Bronowski

"If it dies, it's biology; if it blows up, it's chemistry; if it doesn't work, it's physics."[56]

—John Wilkes

Section 5-1: The Legal Memo— Legal Writing to Inform

Scientists form and test hypotheses about the physical world in order to logically explain phenomena that occur in it. This testing occurs through experimentation, and with each experiment, scientists add to and advance our knowledge of the world around us. Scientific knowledge is derived from empirical study, meaning that all experiments must be based on what is observable and all experiments must be replicable by other scientists working under like conditions. The validity of a scientific hypothesis is proved or disproved based on whether the results are the same when the experiment is duplicated.

---

55. Bruce Peterson, *In Search of Meaning: Readers and Expressive Language*, in LANGUAGE CONNECTIONS: WRITING AND READING ACROSS THE CURRICULUM 120 (Toby Fulwiler & Art Young eds., 1982).

56. John Wilkes, *Science Writing: Who? What? How?* 67 THE ENGLISH JOURNAL 56–60 (Apr. 1978).

In this sense, the construction of scientific knowledge resembles the construction of legal knowledge. Like lawyers, scientists have their own version of *stare decisis*. They treat the results from previous experiments as precedential in the process of building scientific knowledge to the extent that those experiments produce the same results under the same or similar conditions.

Scientists approach the study of the natural world through the "Scientific Method." The Scientific Method requires a scientist to (1) observe a phenomenon in order to identify a problem to explore or other purpose for an experiment; (2) form a hypothesis or theory based on observation; (3) research why the phenomenon occurs or what will occur if the phenomenon is replicated; (4) predict the results of testing the hypothesis; (5) test the hypothesis in an experiment; and (6) analyze the results of the experiment. This process is recorded in several types of writing: the lab notebook and the lab report. A lab notebook is a building block for a lab report.[57] In turn, a lab report is a building block for scientific research paper, although both share similar sections.[58] Scientific research papers in their more polished form become articles.

The Lab Notebook

The standard lab notebook has the following parts:

1. Clear identification of the time, place, and personnel who were directly involved in conducting the experiment.
2. [A short] statement of the problem and purpose of the experiment; the hypothesis or theory it is designed to test.
3. [A short] statement of the predicted results (optional).
4. Detailed descriptions of the apparatus.
5. Detailed instructions for conducting the experiment.
6. Detailed method for collecting data.
7. Complete records of the data on prepared data sheets as well as other observations.
8. [A] [d]escription of the method for analyzing data.
9. [A short] analysis and interpretations of data, including graphs and charts.
10. [A short] statement and conclusions.[59]

---

57. David Porush, A Short Guide to Writing About Science 48–49 (1997).
58. *Id.*
59. *Id.* at 25.

Section 5-2: Reading and Note-taking Strategies for Legal Authorities

In order to actively understand and critically examine the types of texts that scientists write, it is necessary to review the structure of those common texts, their overall rhetorical purpose, and the rhetorical purpose of all of their parts. The overall rhetorical purpose of the lab notebook, lab report, or scientific research paper is to answer a question, to prove or disprove a theory. In developing a notebook, report, and/or article, a scientist follows the Scientific Method to answer a question or to prove or disprove a theory. Each part of the lab notebook has the following rhetorical purpose:

1. **Clear identification of the time, place, and personnel who were directly involved in conducting the experiment.** *Informs the reader of who was present at the experiment and when it took place.*
2. **A short statement of the problem and purpose of the experiment; the hypothesis or theory it is designed to test.** *Focuses the experiment within a broader field of study and defines its scope; gives attribution to the author(s) of the theoretical and methodological underpinnings for the experiment.*[60]
3. **A short statement of the predicted results (optional).** *Tells the reader what to expect from the experiment.*[61]
4. **Detailed descriptions of the apparatus.** *Discusses the apparatus (the means of conducting the experiment) with enough detail so that it can be replicated in future experiments.*[62]
5. **Detailed instructions for conducting the experiment.** *Discusses the instructions in such detail so that the results of the experiment can be replicated by following them.*[63]
6. **Detailed method for collecting data.** *Discusses how data was collected and recorded.*[64]
7. **Complete records of the data on prepared data sheets as well as other observations.** *Illustrates #6.*

---

60. *Id.* at 27; Berkenkotter et al., *supra* note 19, at 196–197.
61. PORUSH, *supra* note 57, at 27.
62. *Id.* at 27–32.
63. *Id.* at 32.
64. *Id.* at 32–37.

8. **Description of the method for analyzing data.** *Discusses the reasons for analyzing data in a certain manner and the processes (e.g. mathematical equations) employed in that analysis.*[65]

9. **A short analysis and interpretations of data, including graphs and charts.** *Gives the reader an interpretation of what the data means by applying a theory or hypothesis.*[66]

10. **A short statement and conclusions.** *Makes judgments about the meaning of the data.*

Just as the structure for scientific notes—notes about observations made in the natural world—is the lab notebook, case briefs are the structure for observing the phenomena that occurs during the judicial process as recorded in cases.

Corresponding Parts of a Lab Notebook, Case, and Case Brief

Parts of a Lab Notebook	Parts of a Case/Case Brief
Identification of time, place, and personnel directly involved in conducting the experiment	Procedural Posture
A short statement of the problem and purpose of the experiment; the hypothesis or theory it is designed to test	Issue
A short statement of the predicted results (*optional*)	Procedural Posture; Ruling
Detailed descriptions of the apparatus	N/A
Detailed instructions for conducting the experiment	N/A
Detailed method for collecting data	N/A
Complete records of the data on prepared data sheets as well as other observations	Facts
Description of the method for analyzing data	Synthesis of Legal Authorities; *Ratio Decidendi*: Synthesis of Legal Authorities
A short analysis and interpretations of data, including graphs and charts	Factual Analysis; *Ratio Decidendi*: Factual Analysis
A short statement and conclusions	Holding

---

65. *Id.* at 37–43.
66. *Id.* at 43–46.

MATERIALS: An example of a lab notebook labeled with the corresponding parts of a case brief is in the Reading and Note-taking folder located in the Exercises & Materials for this chapter as *Lab Notebook for Prediction and Measurement of Volume Flow Rate.*

EXERCISE 1: Label one of the cases in your case file with the parts that correspond to the parts of a lab notebook. After you have labeled the case, brief it according to the instructions in Chapter 1, Section 1-2.

Scientists use lab notebooks for the basic purpose of recording observations and experiments. In this sense, the lab notebook is a tool, a type of template, used to produce a report of experiments conducted rather than a polished piece of writing. The lab report and research paper/article are the polished pieces of writing that emerge out of the lab notebook. The parts of a lab report and research paper/article and the rhetorical purpose of each follow:[67]

1. **Letter of Transmittal.** *Included in lab reports that will be transmitted to a party outside the institution where the experiment was created or to a person inside the institution that is outside of the transmitter's department. Briefly communicates the nature of the experiment and the results.*
2. **Title/Cover Page.** *Identifies what experiment was conducted and those parties involved with conducting it.*
3. **Abstract or Executive Summary.** *Briefly discusses the purpose, methods, results, and conclusion parts of the report.*
4. **Table of Contents.** *Outlines all of the parts of the report. May or may not be included in the research paper/article.*
5. **Introduction/Statement of the Problem.** *Developed from the lab notebook. Sets out the problem explored and reason(s) for its importance. Situates the experiment in the context of the same or similar experiments conducted in the field.*
6. **Hypothesis or Expected Outcome.** *"States [and explains] the hypothesis, theory[,] or theorem the experiment is designed to prove";*[68] *states the expected outcome of the experiment. Also called the "hypotheses, models[,] and theories" (HMT) section.*[69] *Located in or flows from the introduction.*

---

67. *Id.* at 48–62, 65–67.
68. *Id.* at 56.
69. *Id.* at 98.

7. **Literature Review.** *Included in each part of the report or at the beginning. Discusses the disciplinary context of the experiment and the basis of the hypothesis, theory, or theorem on which the experiment is based. Flows out of or is included in #5.*

8. **Methods/Materials.** *Developed from the lab notebook. Discusses the method in more detail than in the lab notebook, cites to the basis for those methods if not original.*

9. **Interpretations of Data/Conclusions.** *Developed from the lab notebook. Presents and gives meaning to the data; a defense of experiment results. [This section is often titled "Results/Discussion" or "Discussion."]*

10. **Sketches of Apparatus and Other Illustrations.** *Developed from the lab report. A more polished refined presentation of this information than what appears in the lab notebook; additional information of the same type.*

11. **Conclusion.** *Developed from the lab notebook. Discusses conclusions in more detail than in the lab notebook. Also gives tips for how further research should be conducted.*

12. **Bibliography of Literature Cited.** *Provides a reader with a comprehensive list of the cited authorities.*

13. **Nomenclature/Glossary.** *Defines the words used in the experiment relating to the procedures and theories in the report.*

14. **Appendices.** *Contains ancillary information that is useful in understanding the report.*

Just as case briefs serve as the foundation for building the legal memo, lab notebooks serve as the foundation for developing lab reports, and lab reports serve as the foundation for developing articles. All of the parts of a lab notebook are found in the lab report and article, just as all of the parts of a legal authority or case are found in the legal memo. The lab report and article borrow from the lab notebook, both in the organization of information and its content, but they also require the author to more fully develop the information in it. Likewise, the legal author must further develop the case brief with supplemental notes and then organize the information into an outline to prepare to write the legal memo. See the correspondence charts on the following pages.

MATERIALS: Examples of a lab report and science article labeled with the corresponding parts of a legal memo are in the Reading and Note-taking folder located in the Exercises & Materials for this chapter as Lab Report #1: *Cross Cannizzaro Reaction: Synthesis of p-Chlorobenzyl Alcohol*; and Article #1: *Long-Term Effects of Temporal Lobe Epilepsy on Local Neural Networks: A Graph Theoretical Analysis of Corticography Recordings.*

Corresponding Parts of a Lab Notebook, Lab Report, and Science Article

Parts of a Lab Notebook	Parts of a Lab Report and Science Article
Identification of time, place, and personnel directly involved in conducting the experiment.	Letter of Transmittal
A short statement of the problem and purpose of the experiment; the hypothesis or theory it is designed to test	Abstract or Executive Summary; Introduction *(including literature review and HMT sections)*
A short statement of the predicted results *(optional)*	Abstract or Executive Summary; Introduction *(including literature review and HMT sections)*
Detailed descriptions of the apparatus	Sketches of Apparatus and Other Illustrations
Detailed instructions for conducting the experiment	Methods and Materials
Detailed method for collecting data	Methods and Materials
Complete records of the data on prepared data sheets as well as other observations	Interpretations of Data/Conclusions
Description of the method for analyzing data	Methods and Materials
A short analysis and interpretations of data, including graphs and charts	Abstract or Executive Summary; Interpretations of Data/Conclusions
A short statement and conclusions	Abstract or Executive Summary; Interpretations of Data/Conclusions

EXERCISE 2: Label Lab Report #2: *The Synthesis of Lydocaine* and Article #2: *The Influence of Recovery and Training Phases on Body Composition, Peripheral Vascular Function and Immune System of Professional Soccer Players* by identifying the parts that correspond to the parts of a legal memo. Both are in the Reading and Note-taking folder located in the Exercises & Materials for this chapter.

Corresponding Parts of a Lab Report, Science Article, and Legal Memo

Parts of a Lab Report and Science Article	Parts of a Legal Memo
Letter of Transmittal	Short Answer
Title/Cover Page	"RE:" line in the memo heading
Abstract or Executive Summary	Short Answer
Table of Contents	N/A
Introduction	Question Presented
Hypothesis or Expected Outcome	Short Answer
Introduction *(HMT and/or a literature review)*	Discussion Section: Synthesis of Legal Authorities
Methods *(a.k.a. Procedure)*	Discussion Section: Synthesis of Legal Authorities
Interpretations of Data/Conclusions *(a.k.a. "Results/Discussion" or "Discussion")*	Statement of Facts; Discussion; Discussion Section: Factual Analysis
Sketches of Apparatus and Other Illustrations	N/A
Conclusion	Conclusion
Bibliography of Literature Cited	*Bluebook* or *ALWD* citation form
Nomenclature/Glossary	N/A
Appendices	Same *(included rarely and only if necessary)*

EXERCISE 3: Label one of the cases in the Legal Memo Case File with the parts that correspond to the parts of the lab report and research paper/article.

Complete **EXERCISES 4, 5** and **6** in Chapter 1.

Section 5-3: Organizing and Synthesizing Legal Authorities

Organization

In reviewing the example lab reports or articles, you may have noticed that the parts of the report or article serve as the outline for the placement and organization of the information. Within each of the sections, the author organizes the relevant information by category. The categories for the information are determined by the parameters and purpose of the scientist's study. As the scientific author moves to the parts of the report or article that increase in complexity, the author organizes the information according to subject specific categories and then organizes the information within the category according to the concepts that each piece of information expresses.

The most common types of organizational structures for information contained in lab reports and science articles are organization by block and point-by-point. In utilizing the block structure, the scientist first separates the information by authority. Under each authority, the author further sorts the information into the category of information that each discusses and then into the concepts discussed in each category. In drafting a report or article organized by block, the author discusses each authority in turn, explaining the similarities and differences in the categories and concepts as the lab report or article progresses. The author's explanation of the similarities and differences between the authorities requires summaries, paraphrases, and quotations from them.

Under the point-by-point structure, the author separates the essay into categories and then within each category lists the major concepts. For each of the authorities relevant to a particular concept, the writer explains the similarities and differences between them and in doing so summarizes, paraphrases, and/or quotes the authorities. The point-by-point organizational structure is the structure most utilized by attorneys in constructing the synthesis of legal authorities. See sample block and point-by-point outlines on the next two pages.

MATERIALS: Examples of the block and point-by-point outlines above in MindMap form are in the Organization and Synthesis folder located in the Exercises & Materials for this chapter.

Complete **EXERCISE 7** in Chapter 1.

Outline of Lab Report or Article Organized by Block

Topic: Quimits

Introduction or Author's Hypothesis: Although Quimits occur in nature and can be formed synthetically, they are most durable when formed and replicated from a hybrid of organic and synthetic compounds.

Authorities Used: Smith and Jones

Introduction

I. Smith

    A. Quimit Formation (CATEGORY 1)

        1. From Organic Compounds (Concept A)

        2. From Synthetic Compounds (Concept B)

        3. From a Hybrid of Organic and Synthetic Compounds (Concept C)

    B. Quimit Characteristics (CATEGORY 2)

        1. From Organic Compounds (Concept A)

        2. From Synthetic Compounds (Concept B)

        3. From a Hybrid of Organic and Synthetic Compounds (Concept C)

    C. Quimit Replication (CATEGORY 3)

        1. From Organic Compounds (Concept A)

        2. From Synthetic Compounds (Concept B)

        3. From a Hybrid of Organic and Synthetic Compounds (Concept C)

II. Jones

    A. Quimit Formation (CATEGORY 1)

        1. From Organic Compounds (Concept A)

        2. From Synthetic Compounds (Concept B)

        3. From a Hybrid of Organic and Synthetic Compounds (Concept C)

    B. Quimit Characteristics (CATEGORY 2)

        1. From Organic Compounds (Concept A)

        2. From Synthetic Compounds (Concept B)

        3. From a Hybrid of Organic and Synthetic Compounds (Concept C)

    C. Quimit Replication (CATEGORY 3)

        1. From Organic Compounds (Concept A)

        2. From Synthetic Compounds (Concept B)

        3. From a Hybrid of Organic and Synthetic Compounds (Concept C)

Outline of a Lab Report or Research Paper/Article
Section Organized Point-by-Point

Topic: Quimits

Introduction or Author's Hypothesis: Although Quimits occur in nature and can be formed synthetically, they are most durable when formed and replicated from a hybrid of organic and synthetic compounds.

Authorities used: Smith and Jones

Introduction:

I. Quimit Formation (CATEGORY 1)

   A. From Organic Compounds (Concept A)—What does each author say about this concept? What are the similarities and differences between each author's assertions?

   B. From Synthetic Compounds (Concept B)—What does each author say about this concept? What are the similarities and differences between each author's assertions?

   C. From a Hybrid of Organic and Synthetic Compounds (Concept C)—What does each author say about this concept? What are the similarities and differences between each author's assertions?

II. Quimit Characteristics (CATEGORY 2)

   A. From Organic Compounds (Concept A)—What does each author say about this concept? What are the similarities and differences between each author's assertions?

   B. From Synthetic Compounds (Concept B)—What does each author say about this concept? What are the similarities and differences between each author's assertions?

   C. From a Hybrid of Organic and Synthetic Compounds (Concept C)—What does each author say about this concept? What are the similarities and differences between each author's assertions?

III. Quimit Replication (CATEGORY 3)

   A. From Organic Compounds (Concept A)—What does each author say about this concept? What are the similarities and differences between each author's assertions?

   B. From Synthetic Compounds (Concept B)—What does each author say about this concept? What are the similarities and differences between each author's assertions?

   C. From a Hybrid of Organic and Synthetic Compounds (Concept C)—What does each author say about this concept? What are the similarities and differences between each author's assertions?

Synthesis

At its core, science is about observation for the purpose of answering a question and/or to prove or disprove a theory. However, before scientists get to the point of observation, they must first choose a scientific problem to study and then consult the relevant literature on the problem to determine how scientists before them have studied it.[70] It is from this research process that the scientist refines the problem and designs an experiment to test and/or gain more information about the problem and possible solutions for it. By recording the processes of experimentation and observation in lab notebooks, lab reports, and articles, scientists are able to make their findings available to other researchers studying the same problems. As a previous scientist's work becomes part of the literature for a particular problem, other scientists will consult that work to refine their hypothesis and design an experiment to test and/or gain more information about the problem and possible solutions for it.[71]

Although one scientific experiment can begin to explain natural phenomena to us, it is the integration of the sum of results from a number of experiments on a given topic that actually forms the body of scientific knowledge. This integration occurs throughout the lab report and science article, but is usually first introduced in the *Introduction* section of these pieces of writing. Careful reading of the relevant scientific literature on a particular problem allows a scientist to craft an *Introduction*, which situates the paper within the broader spectrum of scientific knowledge, before explaining in detail the theories and hypotheses that make up that knowledge. A scientist drafts an *Introduction* of a lab report and article by using the rhetorical moves that follow:

1. Establishes the field in which the study falls and explains its disciplinary context;
2. Summarizes the relevant research for the subject of study;
3. Creates a space for their research by indicating gaps in the relevant research or by raising questions about the research; and
4. Introduces the study by noting the contribution it will make to the field.[72]

Review the table at the top of the facing page.

A key part of the *Introduction* is the hypothesis. A hypothesis is a prediction of what an experiment will reveal about a phenomenon based on an existing theory about the phenomenon or careful observation of it.[73] In essence, the

---

70. *Id.* at 22.
71. *Id.*
72. Berkenkotter et al., *supra* note 19, at 196.
73. Porush, *supra* note 57, at 99–101.

Corresponding Parts of an Introduction and Legal Memo

Parts of the Introduction	Parts of the Legal Memo
Establishes the field in which the study falls or explains the disciplinary context	Question Presented: Communicates to the reader the area or areas of law that the case involves
Summarizes the relevant research for the subject of the study	Question Presented: Communicates to the reader the particular question that the memo seeks to answer
Creates a space for their research by indicating gaps in the relevant research or by raising questions about that research	Question Presented: Communicates to the reader the facts of the case that are important to resolving the question that the memo seeks to answer
Introduces the study by noting the contribution it will make to the field	Short Answer

hypothesis is a predicted solution to the problem the scientist sets out to study. It is like the *Short Answer* in a legal memo, which is an answer to the question posed in the *Question Presented*. See the table below.

Scientists often draft and/or refine their hypotheses after they have completed an experiment in much the same way lawyers draft a *Short Answer* after they have drafted the conclusion to their legal memos.

As scientists integrate scientific knowledge into a lab report or article, they explain that knowledge and cite the scholars who created it. The explanation and citation of scholarly work may extend throughout the lab report or arti-

Corresponding Parts of a Hypothesis and Short Answer

Hypothesis	Short Answer
Predicts the solution to the problem explored in the experiment	Provides a "Yes" or "No" answer to the question posed in the *Question Presented*
Offers a short explanation of the theory guiding the experiment	Offers a short explanation of the legal concept that forms the basis for evaluating the facts of the case
Succinctly states why the experiment results conform to or disprove the theory	Offers a short statement of how the facts of the case meet or do not meet the criteria for evaluation

cle, to the extent that methods, data sources, or other sources of knowledge used in the experiment are not the experimenter's own. In both lab reports and articles, the author may include a literature review section in lieu of discussing the bulk of scientific authority throughout the paper. Regardless of where discussions of scientific knowledge take place, the purpose is the same—to provide the authority for conducting the experiment or study and to serve as a basic foundation for discussing the results of the experiment or study.

In discussing the various types and sources of scientific knowledge, scientists first define the subject of the experiment or study; explain the strengths and weaknesses in how other scientists have approached the same or similar subjects; compare and contrast the points of consonance and dissonance; and then explain how and why their approach is the same as or different from previous approaches used to study their subject.[74] This is similar to the process that an attorney goes through in synthesizing legal authorities by defining the category in which the legal authorities fall and the concepts within those categories; comparing and contrasting the similarities and differences between the authorities by using the major concepts in the authorities; explaining the similarities and differences between the authorities and how they impact our understanding of subsequent authorities; and, finally, connecting all of the explanations.

EXERCISE 4: For Article #2: *The Influence of Recovery and Training Phases on Body Composition, Peripheral Vascular Function and Immune System of Professional Soccer Players,* identify the corresponding parts of the legal memo, introduction, and hypothesis. An example is in the Reading and Note-taking folder located in the Exercises & Materials for this chapter as Article #1A: *Long-Term Effects of Temporal Lobe Epilepsy on Local Neural Networks: A Graph Theoretical Analysis of Corticography Recordings.*

Complete **EXERCISE 8** in Chapter 1.

---

74. *Id.* at 104, 109.

Section 5-4: Using Legal Authorities to Analyze Facts and to Develop Conclusions

Analysis

The body of the lab report and article consists of the description, analysis, and interpretation of the data the scientist has collected from one or multiple experiments. The description of the data in this section is like the *Statement of Facts* in the legal memo. It provides the reader with the information for interpretation and analysis in advance of the actual interpretation and analysis.

When a scientist interprets and analyzes data, they derive meaning for the data from the relevant scientific knowledge and then explain how the data fits within that body of knowledge or deviates from it. In essence, the scientific knowledge detailed throughout the lab report or article becomes the framework through which the data is explained. The framework may be adequate for a scientist to interpret and analyze the data from various perspectives that are all feasible. On the other hand, the framework may be inadequate to provide a complete interpretation and analysis of the data. In both cases, it is up to the scientist to advocate for the adoption of particular interpretation as supported by the data and scientific literature.[75]

The interpretation and analysis of scientific data shares many similarities with the factual analysis in which a legal writer engages. In drafting the interpretation and analysis section, scientific writers must decide whether they will organize the section inductively (conclusions followed by reasons) or deductively (reasons leading to conclusions), and how they will give meaning to the data using the scientific authority throughout the report or article. Accordingly, the scientific writer will weave the facts and authorities together, using certain authorities to support the data and explaining why certain authorities do not support the data and why. The scientific writer accomplishes this task as follows:

[1] [Ordering the] presentation of data logically;

[2] [Using] induction and deduction;

[3] [Moving] from the most certain to the least certain parts of the case;

[4] [Describing] all important and non-obvious assumptions;

---

75. *Id.* at 150.

[5] [Explaining] the relative certainty of all the data, or their standard deviations or error calculations;

[6] [Using] phrases that indicate the logical relations between thoughts or facts;

[7] [Avoiding] phrases that characterize the truth of a statement;

[8] [Avoiding] phrases that characterize the assumed knowledge of the reader;

[9] [Avoiding] phrases that color the qualities of an observation;

[10] [Interweaving the] presentation [of data] and discussion [and] interpretation of the data; and

[11] Explicitly [stating] the pivotal questions as questions in the body of [the] argument.[76]

In this sense, the scientific writer goes through the many of the same rhetorical moves as the legal writer in the analysis section of a legal memo. See the table on the opposite page.

MATERIALS: For examples of the rhetorical moves noted in the table above, review the answer to Exercise 2 in the Model Answers folder for this chapter.

The only rhetorical move that the scientific writer makes that is not mirrored by the legal writer is explicitly stating the pivotal questions as questions in the body of the arguments. For the legal memo, questions are reserved for the *Questions Presented* section. Likewise, a lengthy description and presentation of the data in scientific writing finds its counterpart in the *Statement of Facts* in legal writing.

Complete **EXERCISES 9** and **10** in Chapter 1.

Developing Conclusions

At the conclusion of a lab report or article, the scientist states their conclusions narrowly or broadly (as the evidence supports) and compares and contrasts those conclusions with others that are relevant to their study. The conclusion also is an opportunity for the scientist to discuss matters unresolved by their study of a particular phenomenon and to place the study in the realm

---

76. *Id.* at 163.

Corresponding Rhetorical Moves for Drafting Analysis
Sections in Scientific and Legal Writing

Scientific Analysis and Interpretation	Legal Analysis and Interpretation
Using induction or deduction	Deciding whether to use inductive or deductive reasoning
Ordering the presentation of data logically	Categorizing the facts under the same categories used in the synthesis of authorities
Moving from the most certain to the least certain parts of the case; Describing all important non-obvious assumptions; Explaining the relative certainty of all the data, or their standard deviations or error calculations; Interweaving the presentation of data and discussion/interpretation of the data	Comparing and contrasting the facts in the case with the facts in the legal authorities by concept and category
Moving from the most certain to the least certain parts of the case; Describing all important non-obvious assumptions; Explaining the relative certainty of all the data, or their standard deviations or error calculations; Interweaving the presentation of data and discussion/interpretation of the data	Explaining the relationships between those comparisons using the language of the synthesis of authorities
Using phrases that indicate the logical relations between thoughts or facts; Avoiding phrases that characterize the truth of a statement; Avoiding phrases that characterize the assumed knowledge of the reader; Avoiding phrases that color the qualities of the observation	Connecting all of the explanations moving from point to point, assertion to assertion until all of the plausible explanations are exhausted for and against your side

of like studies in the field as described in the introductory portions of the report or article.[77]

The scientific conclusion is similar to the conclusion at the end of a legal memo. In drafting the *Conclusion*, the legal writer states the conclusion narrowly or broadly, as dictated by the *Question Presented*; states the authority for the conclusion as explained in the synthesis of authorities; and explains how the facts conform with or deviate from the framework for analysis set by the rule syn-

---

77. *Id.* at 164–173.

thesis. Sometimes an attorney will be asked to discuss the next actions to take or to describe information that is unknown at the time the memo was written.

PUTTING IT ALL TOGETHER:

Using the skills that you have learned for building a legal memo, complete the legal memo assignment for the case file assigned to you.

Section 5-5: The Legal Brief— Legal Writing to Persuade

"Scientific publications are seen as persuasive briefs for claims seeking communal validation as knowledge."[78]

—Charles Bazerman

Before beginning to read this section, review the Legal Brief Case File in the Exercises & Materials for Chapter One.

Complete **EXERCISES 11** and **12** in Chapter 1.

Organization

Note that in legal writing the rhetorical purpose of the legal memo is to inform while the rhetorical purpose of the legal brief is to persuade. In the scientific disciplines, the only purely informational type of writing is the lab notebook in which scientists note their observations. The lab report and article, while appearing to present information neutrally and objectively, actually advocate for the adoption of a particular hypothesis, model, or theory (HMT) as supported by existing scientific authority and the data from a particular experiment or study. Thus, the majority of scientific writing is (by design) persuasive writing.

In Sections 5-2 and 5-3, we reviewed parts of science articles for their organizational structure. Revisit any of the articles used in Sections 5-2 and 5-3

---

78. Charles Bazerman, *How Natural Scientists Can Cooperate: The Literacy Technology of Coordinated Investigation in Joseph Priestly's History and Present State of Electricity (1767)*, *in* TEXTUAL DYNAMICS OF THE PROFESSIONS *supra* note 19, at 13.

not only to re-examine their organizational structure, but also to note how the author structures their argument(s). Notice how all of the topic sentences for each major point supports the author's hypothesis. Also notice how the support for the points reference key portions of the scientific authority that informs the study. The topic sentences are like the argumentative point headings in the legal brief. The support for the points is like the persuasive synthesis of authorities and analysis/argument in a legal brief. In the persuasive synthesis of authorities, the legal author sets out the key sources that form the framework for analysis, much like the scientific author does in both explaining and referencing the applicable scientific authority. In the analysis/argument section of the legal brief, the author uses that framework to evaluate the facts of the client's case in the same manner the scientist uses scientific authority to analyze the results of an experiment or experiments in the *Interpretation of Data/Conclusions* section of the lab report and article.

Corresponding Parts of a Lab Report, Science Article, and Legal Brief

Parts of a Lab Report and Science Article	Parts of a Legal Brief
Letter of Transmittal	N/A
Title/Cover Page	Notice of Motion or Cover Sheet
Table of Contents	Table of Contents
Introduction	Introduction
Hypothesis or Expected Outcome	Introduction
Introduction *(literature review)*	Argument: Persuasive Rule Synthesis
Methods	Argument: Persuasive Rule Synthesis
Interpretation of Data/Conclusions *(a.k.a. "Results/Discussion" or "Discussion")*	Statement of Facts; Argument: Factual Analysis/Argument
Sketches of Apparatus and Other Illustrations	N/A
Conclusion	Conclusion
Bibliography of Literature Cited	Table of Authorities
Nomenclature/Glossary	N/A
Appendices	Same *(if necessary)*

MATERIALS: An example of a scientific article labeled with the parts of a legal brief is in the Reading and Note-taking folder located in the Exercises & Materials for this chapter as Article #1B: *Long-Term Effects of Temporal Lobe Epilepsy on Local Neural Networks: A Graph Theoretical Analysis of Corticography Recordings.*

EXERCISE 5: For Article #2: *The Influence of Recovery and Training Phases on Body Composition, Peripheral Vascular Function and Immune System of Professional Soccer Players*, identify the parts that correspond to the parts of the legal brief.

Complete **EXERCISE 13** in Chapter 1.

Synthesis

As discussed previously, the heart of scientific study is observation for the purpose of answering a question and/or to prove or disprove a theory. In writing a lab report or article, authors choose their sources of authority carefully based on the scientific conversation or discourse they seek to enter concerning natural phenomena. Regardless of whether the scientist agrees with certain scientific authorities or develops an HMT that breaks with commonly held beliefs about the natural world, the scientific author must engage the authors who have covered the same or similar topics. Full, comprehensive engagement with scientific authorities requires an author to anticipate the multiple ways that the authorities can be read and to utilize those sources strategically to either emphasize the portions that support a particular hypothesis or theory and de-emphasize portions that do not. The author may emphasize key portions of the text by placing summaries, paraphrases, or quotes of it in prominent places in the paper or report or by repeating key phrases from the research texts that directly support the thesis. In emphasizing and de-emphasizing authority, authors must make some important decisions about how they will explain authority that contradicts their own hypothesis or theory in a manner that continues to provide support for this hypothesis or theory. In reviewing any of the articles in this chapter, note how the author constructs a persuasive synthesis of the scientific literature to support his or her hypothesis.

Complete **EXERCISE 14** in Chapter 1.

Analysis and Conclusions

When scientists analyze the results of an experiment or group of experiments, they evaluate the results using the HMTs as a framework. This process is already persuasive in nature, as the scientist uses the *Interpretation of Data/Conclusions* to provide empirical support for the HMTs presented. This analytical process is the same as the one detailed in Chapter One, Section 1-4 and in Section 5-4 with two key differences. Those differences are noted in **<u>bold and underlined</u>** on the table on the next page.

Just as when the writers of the scientific articles for this chapter decided to strategically emphasize and de-emphasize the parts of scientific authority they discussed to support a particular hypothesis, the writers also emphasized the experiment results that supported their hypotheses and de-emphasized those that did not. Like legal writers, scientific writers use the full weight of the authority to support research findings that adhere to their HMTs as well as to refute those that do not.

Complete **EXERCISES 15** and **16** in Chapter 1.

PUTTING IT ALL TOGETHER:
Using the skills that you have learned for constructing a legal brief, complete the legal brief assignment for the case file assigned to you.

Section 5-6: Exercises & Materials List

This section corresponds to the Exercises & Materials folder located on the CD-ROM that accompanies this text. The following folders and their contents are located within the Exercises & Materials folder for this chapter:

Reading and Note-taking

1. *Lab Notebook for Prediction and Measurement of Volume Flow Rate* (labeled with the parts of a case brief)

2. Lab Report #1: *Cross Cannizzaro Reaction: Synthesis of p-Chlorobenzyl Alcohol* (labeled with the parts of a legal memo)

Corresponding Rhetorical Moves for Drafting Persuasive Analysis/Argument Sections in Scientific and Legal Writing

Scientific Analysis and Interpretation	Persuasive Legal Analysis and Interpretation
Using induction or deduction	Deciding whether to use inductive or deductive reasoning. <u>The reasoning style determines how the topic sentences under each point heading will be constructed</u>
Ordering the presentation of data logically	Categorizing the facts under the same categories used in the synthesis of authorities
Moving from the most certain to the least certain parts of the case; Describing all important non-obvious assumptions; Explaining the relative certainty of all the data, or their standard deviations or error calculations; Interweaving the presentation of data and discussion/interpretation of the data	Comparing and contrasting the facts in the case with the facts in the legal authorities by concept and category
Moving from the most certain to the least certain parts of the case; Describing all important non-obvious assumptions; Explaining the relative certainty of all the data, or their standard deviations or error calculations; Interweaving the presentation of data and discussion/interpretation of the data	Explaining the relationships between those comparisons using the language of the synthesis of authorities
Using phrases that indicate the logical relations between thoughts or facts; Avoiding phrases that characterize the truth of a statement; Avoiding phrases that characterize the assumed knowledge of the reader; Avoiding phrases that color the qualities of the observation	Connecting all of the explanations moving from point to point, assertion to assertion until all of the plausible explanations are exhausted <u>for your side</u>

3.   Article #1: *Long-Term Effects of Temporal Lobe Epilepsy on Local Neural Networks: A Graph Theoretical Analysis of Corticography Recordings* (labeled with the parts of a legal memo)

4.   Lab Report #2: *The Synthesis of Lydocaine*

5.   Article #2: *The Influence of Recovery and Training Phases on Body Composition, Peripheral Vascular Function and Immune System of Professional Soccer Players*

6.   Article #1A: *Article #1 labeled with the parts of a legal memo, introduction, and hypothesis*

7.   Article #1B: *Article #1 labeled with the parts of a legal brief*

Organization and Synthesis

1.   Science MindMap (Point by Point)

2.   Science MindMap (Block)

Chapter Six

Legal Writing from a Business Student's Perspective

"Stop looking for solutions to problems and start looking for the right path."[79]

—Andy Stanley

"[How to think about a problem:] The first step is to make the problem specific ... ; The second step is to form theories freely of how to rid yourself of that burden ... ; The third step is to develop in foresight the consequences of your proposals ... ; The fourth and final step in thinking is to compare the consequences of your proposals to see which is best in the light of your scheme of life as a whole ... ; Whether you choose a vacation or a spouse, a party or a candidate, a cause to contribute to or a creed to live by—think!"[80]

—Brand Blanshard

Section 6-1: The Legal Memo— Legal Writing to Inform

Business professionals are not only charged with inspiring and motivating people to achieve a vision but also with managing human and material resources effectively in service to the vision. Whether impassioned by their own vision, or fueled by the possibility of serving the vision of another, students enter undergraduate and graduate business programs to learn leadership and management skills. Foundational to both skill sets is the ability to problem-solve. The basic business school curriculum is composed of courses on management, management information systems, accounting, ethics, business law, econom-

---

79. Leading Thoughts, http://www.leadershipnow.com/probsolvingquotes.html (last visited Jul. 19, 2011).

80. *Id.*

129

ics, finance and finance mathematics, organizational behavior, business statistics, and operations research. Generally, these courses teach various aspects of problem-solving as it relates to various business and organizational structures. Each uses the business case study as a core instructional piece in order to test and develop problem-solving skills.

Although business students write summaries and critiques of articles in business journals and periodicals, reports, letters, financial statements, consumer analyses, and other types of quantitative and qualitative assessments, most of the assignments that they complete are connected in some way to business case studies designed to evaluate their understanding of how the different aspects of business function. For example, a student may be asked to provide a short answer or write a report in response to a prompt about how to resolve a personnel or organizational issue. Such an assignment utilizes aspects of a real or fictitious business to allow the student to practice, develop, and demonstrate problem-solving skills. Because the processes required to work through business case studies most closely resemble legal writing and analytical processes, a closer examination of them is required.

Section 6-2: Reading and Note-taking Strategies for Legal Authorities

Reading

In short, a business case study presents a problem or set of problems that require solving. The case study itself illustrates a real or simulated situation that requires action. It allows students to apply the theories learned in their business classes to decide the best course of action to take.[81] At its most basic level, a case study is a story. Its rhetorical purpose is to present a problem for solution. A business student must both know and anticipate the parts of the story to deeply engage with the text through questions and note-taking, and to understand the full breadth of the problem that requires solving. The common parts of a case study are as follows:[82]

---

81. Anne Harleman Stewart, *The Role of Narrative Structure in the Transfer of Ideas: The Case Study and Management Theory*, in TEXTUAL DYNAMICS IN THE PROFESSIONS *supra* note 19, at 120–121.

82. LOUISA A. MAUFETTE-LEENDERS, JAMES A. ERSKINE & MICHIEL R. LEENDERS, LEARNING WITH CASES 37 (4th ed. 2007).

[1] The Opening Paragraph[s]: *Identifies for the name and location of the organization, the decision-maker and issue presented, and where the scenario occurs.*[83]

[2] Organization Background (Structure, Products, Industry, Competition, Services, History, Financial Situation): *Provides information on the organization and sometimes places it in an industry context.*[84]

[3] Specific Area of Interest (Marketing, Finance, Operations, Other): *Discusses in detail the specific organizational area where the situation occurs as well as the decision-maker's knowledge, skills, abilities and responsibilities.*[85]

[4] Specific Problem or Decision: *Elaborates on the issue presented in the opening paragraph.*[86]

[5] Alternatives (Optional): *A description of possible alternatives to the problem or decision presented.*

[6] Conclusion (Task, Deadline): *Re-iteration of the task and any time constraints in which the decision must be made.*

A case study also may include various exhibits that are referenced throughout.[87]

Corresponding Parts of a Business Case Study and Legal Case

Parts of a Business Case Study	Parts of a Legal Case
Opening Paragraphs	Procedural Posture; Issue(s)
Organization Background *(Structure, Products, Industry, Competition, Services, History, Financial Situation)*	Procedural Posture; Facts
Specific Area of Interest *(Marketing, Finance, Operations, Other)*	Procedural Posture; Facts
Specific Problem or Decision	Issue(s)
Alternatives *(Optional)*	Facts
Conclusion *(Task, Deadlines)*	Issue(s)

---

83. *Id.* at 38.
84. *Id.*
85. *Id.* at 39.
86. *Id.*
87. *Id.* at 40.

EXERCISE 1: Label Business Case Study #1: *Considering Profits and Principles in Technology Adoption Decisions (A)* by identifying the parts that correspond to the parts of a case. Business Case Study #1 is in the Reading and Note-taking folder located in the Exercises & Materials for this chapter.

EXERCISE 2: Label one of the cases in your case file with the parts that correspond to the parts of the business case study.

Note-taking

As conscientious business students take notes on a case study, they identify the major people involved in the case, the source of the problem or problems, when the problems arose, and possible reasons why the problems occurred.[88] These observations allow the reader to (1) thoroughly explore the issues that the case involves; (2) evaluate and sort the information given in the case to determine what is relevant and what further information is needed; (3) examine the principle concepts, theories and techniques required to resolve the problems that the case presents; (4) consider possible solutions (alternatives) to the issues based on those concepts, theories and techniques; (5) evaluate those alternatives using certain decision criteria and select the best alternative(s); and (6) make a plan to implement those alternatives.[89] This critical engagement with the text finds its parallel in legal note-taking and case briefing as follows:

---

88. *Id.* at 12–16, 34.

89. *Id.* at 12–16; James Erskine, Michiel R. Leenders & Louise A. Maufette-Leenders, Teaching with Cases 141 (1981).

Strategies for Engaging with a Business Case Study	Parts of a Case Brief
Explore the issues *(a.k.a. problems and decisions)* that the case involves	Procedural Posture; Issue
Evaluate and sort the information given in the case to determine what is relevant and what further information is needed	Facts; *Ratio Decidendi*: Factual Analysis
Examine the principle concepts, theories, and techniques required to resolve the problems that the case presents	*Ratio Decidendi*: Rule Synthesis
Consider possible solutions *(alternatives)* to the issues *(problems and decisions)* using the concepts, theories, and techniques	*Ratio Decidendi*: Factual Analysis
Evaluate the alternatives by using certain decision criteria *(such as company ethics and goodwill or profits and cost[90])* and select the best alternative	*Ratio Decidendi*: Factual Analysis; Holding
Make a plan to implement the alternatives	Ruling

EXERCISE 3: For Business Case Study # 1: *Considering Profits and Principles in Technology Adoption Decisions (A)*, make notes using strategies for engaging with a case study. After you have finished, label your notes by identifying the parts that correspond to the parts of case brief.

Complete **EXERCISES 4**, **5** and **6** in Chapter 1.

---

90. MAUFETTE-LEENDERS ET AL., *supra* note 82, at 46 (Exhibit 3-6: List of Common Decision Criteria).

Section 6-3: Organizing and Synthesizing Legal Authorities

Organization

While the initial task of solving the problems presented by the case study is a critical reading of the case itself, the second part is the actual analysis of those problems to determine possible solutions. In analyzing the problem, the business professional must categorize information based on the ultimate structure and content required for the case analysis just as a lawyer organizes information for the different genres of legal writing. The typical case study analysis requires the problem-solver to work through these steps:

A) [D]efine the issue [both those specific to the case and those implicated by it][;]

B) [A]nalyze the case data with focus on causes and effects as well as constraints and opportunities[;]

C) [G]enerate alternatives[;]

D) [S]elect decision criteria[;]

E) [A]ssess alternatives[;]

F) [S]elect the preferred alternative[;] and

G) [D]evelop an action and implementation plan.[91]

Any writing assignment that you were given as a business student may have required some or all of these steps. See the table on the next page.

EXERCISE 4: For Case Study Analysis #1: Considering Profits and Principles in Technology Adoption Decisions (B), identify how the author completes steps A–G above. Label those steps with the corresponding parts of a legal memo. Case Study Analysis #1 is in the Organization and Synthesis folder located in the Exercises & Materials for this chapter.

Complete **EXERCISE 7** in Chapter 1.

---

91. *Id.* at 40.

Corresponding Parts of a Business Case Analysis and Legal Memo

Parts of a Business Case Analysis	Parts of a Legal Memo
Define the Issue	Question Presented
Analyze the case data with focus on causes and effects as well as constraints and opportunities	Discussion Section: Factual Analysis
Generate alternatives	Statement of Facts
Select decision criteria	Discussion Section: Synthesis of Legal Authorities
Assess alternatives	Discussion Section: Factual Analysis
Select the preferred alternative	Short Answer; Conclusion
Develop an action and implementation plan	Conclusion (*if it includes an "Actions to Take" section*)

Synthesis

In working through a case study, a business professional synthesizes the information from various theories, models, and other analytical tools in order to develop a framework by which to analyze case data. The theories, models, and other analytical tools used to develop the framework for analysis are tied to the specific subject area of the case study.[92] Identifying and synthesizing the applicable theories, models, and other analytical tools is often a key aspect of the case study and takes considerable time. Without it, it is virtually impossible for a business professional to analyze the case data effectively.

In any given business program, students may be asked to present information in a case study analysis in verbal and/or written form. Regardless of the manner the information is communicated, a business student or business professional must follow the analytical process detailed above. A case analysis in written form generally has these parts:

1. Title Page
2. Table of Contents
3. Executive Summary
4. Problem or Issue Statement

---

92. *Id.* at 44.

5. Data Analysis
6. Key Decision Criteria
7. Alternative Analysis
8. Recommendations
9. Action [&] Implementation Plan
10. Exhibits[93]

While the characteristics of written business case study analyses may vary, items 4–9 constitute the bulk of any analysis.[94] The *Title Page* and *Table of Contents* serve to orient the reader to the layout of the analysis while the *Executive Summary* gives the reader a sense of the major decisions and alternatives that the analysis engages.

As noted in the table above, the *Data Analysis, Key Decision Criteria,* and *Alternative Analysis* sections in a written case analysis are most like the *Discussion Section* of the legal memo. In particular, the theories, models, and other analytical tools used to create the framework for analyzing the data, and the decision criteria used to evaluate the alternatives are like the synthesis of legal authorities in a legal memo. The theories, models, and other analytical tools give the business professional the ability to make both qualitative and quantitative assessments of a business problem in terms of its causes and effects, the constraints and opportunities (determined by company resources) that form the boundaries for any decision making process, and then to generate viable alternatives to resolve the problem.[95] The decision criteria facilitate the business professional's decision between viable alternatives to solve the problem.[96]

Essentially, the process of synthesizing information in order to form a framework for analysis is about matching the appropriate analytical tool (theory, model, etc.) to the relevant problem and then using the tool to generate alternatives. For example, if confronted with the problem of poor employee morale, a manager may want to consult and synthesize information about internal and external motivation factors that influence employee morale. In writing a report on the same issue, the manager would discuss the information gleaned from various resources by comparing and contrasting them to each other, and then use that information to generate the alternatives that would be assessed in the

---

93. Introduction to Business 2006, http://socrates.acadiau.ca/courses/Busi/IntroBus/ CaseMethod.html (last visited Jul. 19, 2011).
94. Erskine et al., *supra* note 89, at 217–218.
95. Maufette-Leenders et al., *supra* note 82, at 44–45.
96. *Id.* at 47–48.

Alternative Analysis section of the report. This process is accomplished by clear organization of the information that is being discussed and then by summarizing and paraphrasing from the sources of the information to highlight points of agreement, disagreement, and resolution of the disagreements. Information in the *Data Analysis, Key Decision Criteria,* and *Alternative Analysis* sections is usually organized according to subject heading.

Revisit your work for Exercise 4 above. Note how the authors of Case Study Analysis #1 use various sources of information to build an analytical framework for the case data and then generate alternatives.

Complete **EXERCISE 8** in Chapter 1.

Section 6-4: Using Legal Authorities to Analyze Facts and to Develop Conclusions

Analysis

The analysis process in a legal memo is akin to the generation of alternatives that occurs in the *Data Analysis* section of the written case evaluation, and the assessment of alternatives that occurs in the *Key Decision Criteria* and *Alternative Analysis* sections. The analysis process in both sections is an interpretation and evaluation of the key data in the business case (facts, statistics, etc.) in the context of an applicable analytical framework and decision criteria for the purpose of resolving a particular problem. In applying the analytical framework to the case data in a written business case analysis, it is unacceptable for the business professional to just recount large chunks of the facts. Rather, the case analyst demonstrates how case data are supported by the analytical framework and how they are not, and then uses that evaluation to generate alternative solutions to the problem. In the *Key Decision Criteria* and *Alternative Analysis* sections, the case analyst assesses the alternative solutions according to the essential decision criteria for the organization. This process is most similar to the analytical process that occurs in a legal brief, so a detailed discussion of it is reserved for that section.

Developing Conclusions

The *Recommendations* and *Action & Implementation Plan* sections in a written case analysis are where business professionals select the best alternatives and decide the manner they will be implemented in the organization. These sections are the same as the formal conclusion in a legal memo, where the legal writer discusses the most probable outcome(s) for the client's case and then sets out any further actions that need to be taken.

Complete **EXERCISES 9** and **10** in Chapter 1.

PUTTING IT ALL TOGETHER:
Using the skills that you have learned for building a legal memo, complete the legal memo assignment for the case file assigned to you.

Section 6-5: The Legal Brief— Writing to Persuade

"Management is efficiency in climbing the ladder of success; leadership determines whether the ladder is leaning against the right wall."[97]
—Stephen R. Covey

Before beginning to read this section, review the Legal Brief Case File in the Exercises & Materials for Chapter One.

Complete **EXERCISES 11** and **12** in Chapter 1.

Organization

As mentioned previously, the rhetorical purpose of the business case study and business case study analysis is to place a business student in a typical busi-

---

97. Thinkexist.com Quotations, http://thinkexist.com/quotation/management_is_efficiency_in_climbing_the_ladder/220119.html (last visited Jul. 19, 2011).

ness scenario for the purpose of evaluating their decision-making and analytical problem-solving abilities. While on its face the entire business case study analysis may appear to be objective and informational, it does contain parts that are arguably persuasive. These parts are the *Key Decision Criteria* and *Alternative Analysis* sections. The decision criteria that a business professional utilizes to determine the best course of action for an organization are determined by the values and goals of the organization. For example, if an organizational brand is shaped by its commitment to the environment, then a key decision criterion will always be the environmental impact of any given alternative to resolve a problem. If a viable alternative preserves the organization's commitment to the environment but undermines other key decision criteria, such as profit and cost, then the decision-maker must explore other alternatives that preserve all of the key decision criteria or advocate for why a certain criterion takes priority over others in that particular instance.

This is similar to what a legal writer does in persuasively synthesizing legal authorities and developing arguments for their client using that synthesis as an analytical framework. Because it would be careless and disingenuous for a business professional to cast the analytical framework in a manner that minimizes information that is not favorable to the organization, the *Data Analysis* section remains an objective piece of writing like a legal memo. However, that professional's identification and prioritization of key decision criteria is a subjective process that may require advocacy for a particular course of action deemed by the professional to be necessary for the health of the organization. Accordingly, the *Key Decision Criteria* and *Alternative Analysis* sections find parallels in the legal brief. See the table on the next page.

Again, in analyzing a business problem, the business professional must categorize information based on the ultimate structure and content required for the case analysis just as a lawyer organizes information for the different genres of legal writing.

EXERCISE 5: For Business Case Study Analysis #1, label the parts as they correspond to the parts of a legal brief.

Complete **EXERCISE 13** in Chapter 1.

Corresponding Parts of a Written Case Analysis and Legal Brief

Parts of a Written Business Case Analysis	Parts of a Legal Brief
Title Page	Notice of Motion or Cover Sheet
Table of Contents	Table of Contents
Problem or Issue Statement	Introduction
Executive Summary	Introduction; Conclusion and Prayer for Relief
Data Analysis	Statement of Facts; Argument: Persuasive Rule Synthesis
Decision Criteria	Motion Standard of Review; Argument: Synthesis of Legal Authorities
Alternative Analysis	Argument: Factual Analysis/Argument
Recommendations	Conclusion and Prayer for Relief
Action and Implementation Plan	N/A
Exhibits	Same (*if necessary*)

Synthesis

In the persuasive synthesis of authorities, the legal author sets out the key sources that form the framework for analysis. However, in the *Alternative Analysis* section of a case study analysis, the author persuades the reader of the priority of key decision criteria by strategically evaluating alternatives using the models, theories, and other analytical tools that emphasize certain decision criteria over others. In doing so, the case analyst may emphasize key portions of these models, theories, and other analytical tools by placing summaries, paraphrases, or quotes from them in the written analysis or by repeating key phrases from them that directly support the prioritized decision criteria. Revisit your work for Exercise 5 above. Note how the authors of Case Study Analysis #1 provide justification for prioritizing specific key decision criteria.

Notice how all of the topic sentences for each major point in a section that analyzes the alternatives supports the author's identification and prioritization of the organization's key decision criteria. These topic sentences are similar to the point headings in a legal brief. The support for the points that utilize models, theories, and other analytical tools are like the persuasive synthesis of authorities in the legal brief. The main difference between the two is that the synthesis of legal authorities is stated cohesively by category and concept, while the model, theories, and analytical tools used in the *Alternative Analysis* section are woven throughout the relevant category.

Complete **EXERCISE 14** in Chapter 1.

Analysis and Conclusions

In drafting the *Alternative Analysis* portion of the case analysis, the business professional evaluates alternative solutions to the problem using the decision criteria as well as the analytical tools described above. As mentioned previously, this process is persuasive in that the analyst uses key portions of the case data, viewed through the selected analytical framework, to support the prioritization of the decision criteria. Again, the case analyst emphasizes parts of the case data that support the prioritization of certain decision criteria and de-emphasizes the data that do not. Notice how the authors use the case data, as viewed through the selected analytical framework, in Case Study Analysis #1 to support the prioritization of certain decision criteria.

Complete **EXERCISES 15** and **16** in Chapter 1.

PUTTING IT ALL TOGETHER:
Using the skills that you have learned for constructing a legal brief, complete the legal brief assignment for the case file assigned to you.

Section 6-6: Exercises & Materials List

This section corresponds to the Exercises & Materials folder located on the CD-ROM that accompanies this text. The following folders and their contents are located within the Exercises & Materials folder for this chapter:

Reading and Note-taking

Business Case Study #1: Considering Profits and Principles in Technology Adoption Decisions (A)

Organization and Synthesis

Business Case Study Analysis #1: Considering Profits and Principles in Technology Adoption Decisions (B)

Model Answers List

This section corresponds to the Model Answers folder located on the CD-ROM that accompanies this text. The following folders and their contents are located within the Model Answers folder for each chapter:

Chapter One:
A Discipline-Specific Approach to Legal Writing

Exercise 2 — Statutory Diagram — "Unlawful bear exploitation"

Exercise 4 — Case Briefs for Cases in the Legal Memo Case File

Exercise 5 — Examples of listing, free writing, and cubing (Memo)

Exercise 6 — *(See Nickety Model Memo Annotated)*

Exercise 7 — Sample outline and MindMap (Memo)

Exercise 8 — *(See Nickety Model Memo Annotated)*

Exercise 9 — *(See Nickety Model Memo Annotated)*

Exercise 10 — *(See Nickety Model Memo Annotated)*

Exercise 11 — Case Brief for Legal Authority in the Legal Brief Case File

Exercise 12 — Examples of listing, free writing, and cubing (Legal Brief)

Exercise 13 — Sample outline and MindMap (Legal Brief)

Exercise 14 — *(See Nickety Model Legal Brief Annotated)*

Exercise 15 — *(See Nickety Model Legal Brief Annotated)*

Exercise 16 — *(See Nickety Model Legal Brief Annotated)*

Exercise 18 — Case Briefs for Final Exam Cases

Exercise 20 — Answer to "Who's Joking?"

Exercise 21 — Sample Final Exam Outline and MindMap

Nickety Model Memo

Nickety Model Memo (Annotated)

Nickety Model Legal Brief

Nickety Model Legal Brief (Annotated)

Model Final Exam Answer

Model Final Exam Answer (Annotated)

Chapter Two:
Legal Writing from a Social Scientist's Perspective

Exercise 1—*We Do Not Enjoy Equal Political Rights: Ghanaian Women's Perceptions on Political Participation in Ghana* (labeled with the parts of a legal memo)

Exercise 3—*We Do Not Enjoy Equal Political Rights: Ghanaian Women's Perceptions on Political Participation in Ghana* (labeled with the parts of a case brief and the rhetorical moves for Questions Presented)

Exercise 4—*See Answer for Exercise 7, Chapter One*

Exercise 5—*We Do Not Enjoy Equal Political Rights: Ghanaian Women's Perceptions on Political Participation in Ghana* (labeled with the parts of a legal brief)

Chapter Three:
Legal Writing from a Humanitarian's Perspective

Exercise 1—Analytical Essay #1: *Billy Pilgrim's Motion Sickness: Chronesthesia and Duration in Slaughterhouse-Five* (labeled with parts of a case and legal memo); Analytical Essay #2: *Hol(e)y Statues: Some reflections on holes, emptiness and longing in the work of two Australian émigré sculptors of the fifties* (labeled with parts of a case and legal memo)

Exercise 3—Exegetical Essay #1: *'The Elijah who was to come': Matthew's use of Malachi (Matt 11:2–15)* (labeled with parts of a case and legal memo)

Exercise 5—Explicative Essay #1: *The Off-"Beat" Rhythms and Self-Expression in the Typography and Verse of Ntozake Shange* (labeled with parts of a case and legal memo); *Explicative Essay #2: John Donne's Via Media in 'Satire III"* (labeled with parts of a case and legal memo)

Exercise 7—Argumentative Essay #1: *Get Your Paws Off of My Pixels: Personal Identity and Avatars as Self* (labeled with parts of a case and legal memo)

Exercise 13—Analytical Essay #1 (labeled with the parts of a legal brief); Analytical Essay #2 (labeled with the parts of a legal brief)

Exercise 14—Exegetical Essay #1 (labeled with the parts of a legal brief)

Exercise 15—Explicative Essay #1 (labeled with the parts of a legal brief); Explicative Essay #2 (labeled with the parts of a legal brief)

Exercise 16—Argumentative Essay #2 (labeled with the parts of a legal brief)

Chapter Four:
Legal Writing from an Artist's Perspective
Please Note: There are no model answers for this chapter.

Chapter Five:
Legal Writing from a Scientist's Perspective

Exercise 2—Lab Report #2: *The Synthesis of Lydocaine* (labeled with the parts of a legal memo); Article #2: *The Influence of Recovery and Training Phases on Body Composition, Peripheral Vascular Function and Immune System of Professional Soccer Players* (labeled with the parts of a legal memo)

Exercise 4—Article #2: *The Influence of Recovery and Training Phases on Body Composition, Peripheral Vascular Function and Immune System of Professional Soccer Players* (labeled with the parts of a legal memo, introduction, and hypothesis)

Exercise 5—Article #2: *The Influence of Recovery and Training Phases on Body Composition, Peripheral Vascular Function and Immune System of Professional Soccer Players* (labeled with the parts of a legal brief)

Chapter Six:
Legal Writing from a Business Student's Perspective

Exercise 1—Business Case Study #1: Considering Profits and Principles in Technology Adoption Decisions (A) (labeled with the parts of a case)

Exercise 4—Business Case Study Analysis #1: Considering Profits and Principles in Technology Adoption Decisions (B) (labeled with the parts of a business case analysis and legal memo)

Exercise 5—Business Case Study Analysis #1: Considering Profits and Principles in Technology Adoption Decisions (B) (labeled with the parts of a legal brief)

Index